From the Library of
Bryce Miller

Using Scripture in a Global Age

AF531234

Institute of Mennonite Studies Occasional Papers No. 24

The purpose of the Institute of Mennonite Studies Occasional Papers series is to publish essays by Mennonite scholars, especially those who teach in Mennonite seminaries and colleges, in order to foster conversation in biblical, theological, and practical ministry areas and to invite critical counsel from within the Mennonite theological community. Although most essays will be in finished form, some may also be in a more germinal stage—released especially for purposes of testing and receiving critical response.

Using Scripture in a Global Age

Framing Biblical Issues

C. Norman Kraus
Foreword by John A. Lapp

Institute of Mennonite Studies
Occasional Papers, No. 24

Publishing House
Telford, Pennsylvania

copublished with
Herald Press
Scottdale, Pennsylvania

Cascadia Publishing House orders, information, reprint permissions:
contact@CascadiaPublishingHouse.com
1-215-723-9125
126 Klingerman Road, Telford PA 18969
www.CascadiaPublishingHouse.com

Using Scripture in a Global Age
Copyright © 2006 by Cascadia Publishing House,
Telford, PA 18969
All rights reserved.
Copublished with Herald Press, Scottdale, PA
Library of Congress Catalog Number: 2005036465
ISBN: 1-931038-35-X
Book design by Cascadia Publishing House
Cover design by Merrill R. Miller

The paper used in this publication is recycled and meets the minimum requirements of American National Standard for Information Sciences—Permanence of Paper for Printed Library Materials, ANSI Z39.48-1984.
All Bible quotations are used by permission, all rights reserved and unless otherwise noted are from *The New Revised Standard Version of the Bible*, copyright 1989, by the Division of Christian Education of the National Council of the Churches of Christ in the USA.

Library of Congress Cataloguing-in-Publication Data

Kraus, C. Norman (Clyde Norman), 1924-
Using Scripture in a global age : framing biblical issues / C. Norman Kraus ; foreword by John A. Lapp.
p. cm. -- (Institute of Mennonite Studies occasional papers ; no. 24)
Includes bibliographical references and index.
ISBN-13: 978-1-931038-35-5 (trade pbk. : alk. paper)
ISBN-10: 1-931038-35-X (trade pbk. : alk. paper)
1. Bible--Hermeneutics. 2. Mennonites--Doctrines. 3. Anabaptists--Doctrines. I. Title. II. Series: Occasional papers (Institute of Mennonite Studies (Elkhart, Ind.) ; no. 24.

BS476.K68 2006
220.6088'2897--dc22

2005036465

12 11 10 09 08 07 06 10 9 8 7 6 5 4 3 2 1

To Rhoda:
companion,
interlocutor,
stimulus,
advocate,
and critic

Contents

The Foreword

Journalists are fond of describing massive events—floods, earthquakes, hurricanes—in terms of their "biblical proportions." I've often wondered what that means. Presumably it has to do with size, such as the flood described in the book of Genesis. Or perhaps it has to do with events that change the direction of history. Interestingly, events which loom large on the biblical tapestry generally received little attention in other contemporary accounts.

Such a simple observation indicates that the Bible is in constant need of interpretation and explanation if it is to be useful. More profoundly, the biblical narrative and its significant teachings happen in a time and place remarkably different from twentieth- and twenty-first-century Western society. Some historians describe the past as "a foreign country." Such differences mean that there needs to be constant translation from one situation to another. Needing translation are not only words and sentences but also cultural mores and philosophical presuppositions of one historical epoch into another.

The title of this volume recognizes that a global age requires a new framing of biblical issues. If a tsunami had struck the Indian Ocean in the fifth century before Christ, the people of the Middle East would not have known of the event nor its impact. Not so when the whole world mobilized to alleviate the suffering of the 2004 tsunami victims. Not only did we quickly know about the event, people around the world also responded quickly. European and North American Christian churches immediately asked their co-religionists in Indonesia, Thailand, and India how they were and how we might respond. Europe and North America had the technological, financial, and material resources to move people and goods over long distances and capacities to attend to health, food, and shelter needs. For people in Bible times, such a response could simply not have beemn envisioned.

The word *global* indicates a context unknown in the Bible. Hence for people who regard the Bible as Scripture—texts that reveal who God is and demonstrate what it means to follow the ways of God—there needs to be systematic study, translation, and discernment. Norman Kraus poses the questions well:"How do we read the Scriptures in our global world?" "How do we understand the Bible as authoritative across the multiplicity of cultures?" "How does the acquisition of new knowledge affect the discernment process?"

For sixty years Norman Kraus has been helping the church to develop a deeper understanding of the Scriptures. His first book, published in 1958 by John Knox Press, dealt with biblical materials regarding the future as proposed by *Dispensationalism in America.* This current book summarizes a lifelong concern that students and translators pay more attention to the cultural context not only of those who inhabit the pages of the Scriptures but also the cultural context of writers, translators, and interpreters as well as that of each reader. The reason to exegete "one's own world set in relation to exegesis of the biblical text" is in order "that one can move from text to proclamation." As missionaries in an overseas situation need to contextualize the gospel message, so do pastors, teachers, theologians in twenty-first century North America. We might say that our time is a foreign country to that of biblical times.

In pursuing the task of contextualizing, Kraus deals with a variety of topics: a christocentric hermeneutic, cultural diversity, congregational pluralism, peace and nonviolence, spirituality, sexuality, technology, the shape of the church for the contemporary world. With topics like these, Kraus sometimes treads where readers might become apprehensive. He is a teacher. He likes to provoke thought. He asks for careful consideration and invites thoughtful disagreement.

The real point for Norman Kraus is not merely scholarship. His concern is evangelical. "The goal of Bible study is not theoretical knowledge but practical behavior—justice, peace, and joy in the Holy Spirit." He presents a strong case for an Anabaptist style of interpreting the Scriptures and practices for the church. His pages on "generic anabaptism" do not present Mennonitism writ large. Rather generic anabaptism "represents a post-denominational perspective that seeks to dialogue across denominational lines." The chapters on Anabaptist spirituality and founding an Anabaptist-style congregation plus his stories from Japan highlight meanings for our time. The Assembly Congregation in Goshen, Indiana, illustrates this in goals for worship which, as Kraus reports, are to discover "a true identity as God's people" and find "enablement for authentic discipleship." Indeed a congregation in Anabaptist perspective sees itself as a community participating in the history-long drama of redemption.

Each chapter of *Using Scripture in a Global Age* demonstrates Kraus's passion for serious scriptural study and vital congregational life. Along the way there are critical comments on misreading the Scriptures and inadequate church practice, especially in the concluding autobiographical chapters. Organizational types like myself will occasionally squirm at his critique of institutions. Without squirming and repenting there will be no change or growth.

Every chapter in this volume invites discussion. I hope many people will seize the opportunity of reading this volume to engage in conversations about the urgent issues for the church explored here.

—John A. Lapp, Akron, Pennsylvania, is Executive Secretary Emeritus of Mennonite Central Committee as well as Coordinator of the Global Mennonite History Project for Mennonite World Conference

Introduction: Reading the Bible as Scripture

As I stood in the doorway of the Maple Grove Church in 1951 greeting the congregation after the sermon, I was holding my Revised Standard Version of the Bible, which had been recently published in a hardback red buckram binding. When one of my more elderly church members reached for my hand, he said almost gruffly, "When are you going to get rid of that red book and get a Bible?" Many conservative Christians viewed as heretical this new translation that had dared to present itself as a church sponsored "standard" revision and updating of the King James Version. There were even RSV "Bible burning" protests. Now more than fifty years and dozens of translations and paraphrases later such an uproar over a Bible translation seems almost impossible. Even the more traditional church publishers sponsor every imaginable colloquial version of its text. Yet with all the variety of English versions available, and perhaps partly because of the many versions, reading and applying the biblical message to our contemporary world situation remains highly problematic.

What is it about this Bible that so unites and at the same time separates us Christians? Christians and Jews of all descriptions respect the Bible as "holy Scripture"—that is, as an honored and authoritative book. However, we adopt quite different responses and life styles based on its teaching. Recently in a Jerusalem synagogue service I witnessed genuine reverence for the Torah Scroll with which I could identify, yet I find myself as a Christian responding quite differently to its message. Even within the evangelical Christian tradition there are major variations of interpretation, both in theology and ethics.

For example, currently the theological question of "open theism" is dividing the Evangelical Theological Society. Does the Bible teach that God knows precisely everything that will happen in the future or not? And how shall we discern the proper "biblical" application of the teaching in1 Timothy concerning the ordination of women to the Christian ministry? Or how does one account for the contradictory differences that exist between Christian Zionists, who are able to justify from Scripture the hostility and violence of Israel against its Palestinian neighbors, and those, including Palestinian Christians, who according to Scripture find such behavior ungodly and immoral?

How to read the Scriptures has become a major problem in our global world. How shall we determine their "meaning" for today? What kind of a book is the Bible? Shall we view it as a direct, personal word from God to each individual who reads it? Or is it primarily a book of instructions for the church as it continues the mission of Christ? Is it a magical (Christians prefer the word *supernatural*) book that contains no errors in its original version? The question of the "inerrancy" of the text is still a major concern among the ETS scholars. Is it a historical record of God's self-revelation through Israel? Is it a book of transcultural principles—something like a constitution upon which everyday laws are to be based? And, if so, how is it related to the living self-disclosure we hold came to us in Jesus Christ?

The pluralism not only in our world but also in our churches, along withour global cross-cultural consciousness, requires us to re-examine our rationale for the claims we make about the Bible and the way we use it in the church. Among the sacred Scriptures of the world, the Bible is unique in its historical character, and this has significant implications for the way we read and use it. Hindu Scriptures are mystical and philosophical. Buddhist writings are ethical and mystical in import, while Shinto sacred writings are mythocultural. The Koran claims an oracular origin—that is, its words were dictated by Allah preserved in heaven and represented in the Arabic original on earth. But the Hebrew-Christian Scriptures are historical documents recording Israel's history according to its self-understanding as a covenant people with God as Monarch. God rules over Israel by sending them lawgivers, deliverers, prophets, and finally the Messiah. In this way God's (Yahweh) holy selfhood and will is revealed, and this revelatory history is recorded in the Scriptures.

This "historical" character of the biblical texts affects the way it is applied and used across cultures. Because it is so clearly oriented to a particular culture, the Hebrew, it cannot be read simply in a *trans-cultural* mode. Such a reading might be applied to the Wisdom books that claim to be universal in their perspective. But it cannot be applied to prophetic books like Amos and Zechariah, or to books like Exodus, Leviticus, or Joshua and Judges from the Torah tradition. These books require *cross-cultural* adaptations, and it is precisely this cross-cultural adaptation that we see happening in the pages of the New Testament.

Christians see the life of Jesus, the Messiah, as the fulfillment of this history, and the church of Jesus Christ as the continuation of the mission or movement, which he inaugurated. In a certain sense the story of the Bible continues through the continuing work of the Spirit of Jesus, who is recognized as the Holy Spirit of God. As heir and continuing witness to the revelation recorded in the Bible, the church has defined the parameters of the historical Scripture (canon) with which it identifies, and through the ongoing inspiration of the Spirit interprets and applies (contextualizes) its message in the contemporary age. The Bible has from the beginning been recognized as the book of the church and has been translated and used in cross-cultural mission.

From its beginning the Anabaptist tradition has been Bible-centered rather than theology-centered. It can be argued that the Anabaptist movement of the sixteenth century would not have been possible without the textual work of Erasmus restoring the original Greek text of the New Testament and Martin Luther's translation of the Bible into German. Today Mennonites around the world have begun to reclaim the term *Anabaptist* to describe their distinctive church position and again a biblical rather than a systematic theology has been the unifying factor. But what does this mean? How are we to understand and use the Bible as authoritative Scripture across the multiplicity of cultures in which the Anabaptist tradition has been introduced? Should we expect our Asian and African sisters and brothers to interpret and apply Scripture exactly as we do in the West?

Western Mennonite biblical scholars have diligently exegeted Scripture but have given far less attention to the task of "exegeting" modern cultures and locating the message of the Bible in their contexts. "Discernment" has virtually become a shibboleth in church vocabulary, and discernment involves spiritual insight into its meaning and relevance *for today*. It means more than determining what the ancient text of the Bible meant in its original setting. It requires a discriminating analysis of the contemporary cultural situation into which the Scriptures are translated. It requires *contextualization*.

Put in technical terms, what we need, and thus far have shied away from defining, is a theological hermeneutic that recognizes the freedom of the Holy Spirit to guide the church in interpreting and applying the text of Scripture in the multiplicity of global cultures. Stated in terms of church polity, this will necessitate the location of authority in the body of Christ. Is discernment reserved for an institutional hierarchy of the church? For biblical and theological scholars? For democratic conference decision making structures? Is it the work of the laity in the local congregation?

This book of essays tackles these questions, but not as a sustained rational argument divided into sequential chapters. Rather, it is a collection of essays gathered around a theme. Several of the chapters examine the historical Anabaptist-Mennonite perspective on biblical interpretation and authority. Several more explore the methodological presuppositions of the hermeneutical process and suggest contextualized interpretations in the areas of peace, spirituality, and sexuality. Two of the chapters deal with biblical applications in discipleship and congregational life. And finally, two overlapping autobiographical pieces trace how my mind has changed and the experiences that led me from Mennonite fundamentalism to critical Anabaptism.

Using Scripture in a Global Age

1

Now That "Restrictions" Are Gone

The Mennonite tradition was under severe social pressures in the decades following the Civil War (1865-) through the post-World War I years. In fact, American society itself was in a revolutionary social mode. One can trace these pressures and changes in the Mennonite communities in the minutes of Mennonite church district conferences. Subjects relating to marriage and divorce, relations to the government, implications of the doctrine of nonresistance, dress codes, proper Sunday observance, use of the new self-propelled carriages, voting, use of tobacco and alcoholic beverages, for example, come up for discussion year after year. Leaders became more and more explicit in their regulation of members' social behavior as the era progressed.

It was during these years that the concept of nonconformity to the world was tagged as "restrictions." In the 1898 edition of Daniel Kauffman's *Manual of Bible Doctrines,* chapter nineteen is entitled "Nonconformity to the World," followed by a quotation of Romans 12:2 and a heading "What This Restriction Implies."

Next in 1914 came the edited volume *Bible Doctrine,* with Kauffman as editor, which gave a major section (pp. 459-585) to "Christian Principles, Duties and Restrictions." The duties or obligations were obedience, self-denial, worship, and Christian service defined as "personal work." The restrictions were nonconformity, nonresistance, non-swearing of oaths, non-membership in secret societies, and non-ownership of life insurance. By 1921 the language of restrictions found its way into the Mennonite church's confession of faith as "Article XIII. Of Restrictions" in "Christian Fundamentals, Articles of Faith."[1]

The Way We Were

I have referred to this verbal phenomenon because it illustrates most clearly the way in which church leaders of the period went about interpreting and applying Scripture. For the most part the "restrictions" they enunciated are no longer put into practice. Wearing gold, owning life insurance, the many dress regulations, attendance at county fairs and theaters, participating in political campaigns and voting, divorce and remarriage—all based on "principles" of biblical separation from the world—are no longer taboo. The more attenuated language of *discipleship* has replaced the specific language and applications of nonconformity, and practice differs markedly in the life of the church as a separated community.

Have "principles" changed? If not, what has changed? Clearly the question of hermeneutical method is open for redefinition.

Before we attempt to answer the questions raised above, it might be helpful to reflect on the implicit hermeneutic used by church leaders of the previous century. While they did not explicitly deal with the methodology of interpretation, their writings and manner of problem solving clearly reflect a thoughtful and consistent model.

They read Scripture as an inspired and authoritative record of God's dealing with Israel and the church that included God's instructions and regulations for their life in the world. They understood themselves by way of analogy to be the new Israel of God, therefore the instructions were applied directly to themselves. The oft-quoted text, 2 Timothy 3:16-17, says that Scripture is given "for teaching, for reproof, for correction, and for training in righteousness, so that everyone who belongs to God may be proficient, equipped for every good work."

Accordingly they approached the Bible as a book of divine instructions and rules. The instruction, of course, included doctrine, but the nub of Scripture was not intellectual doctrinal information such as the doctrine of the Trinity, but a worldview and a covenant law for regulating the divine community. At the heart of this covenant law was the teaching and example of Jesus as he was understood and explained in the New Testament writings.

They did not read this record simply as an account of an ancient past but as an ongoing set of regulations for the faithful church in the nineteenth and twentieth centuries. They understood the text of the Bible as addressed to them for the governance of the church. It taught what was necessary for members of the church to believe, and it spelled out the obligations and duties of faithful membership.

Furthermore, they read Scripture as a modern document. This meant in translation—either German or King James English. The jests about one deacon who was sure that the original Bible was written in German because God said, "Adam, *wo bist du*?" or the preacher who avowed that "if the King James Version was good enough for the apostle Paul, it was good enough for him," although exaggerated humor make the point. Words were understood according to their meaning in contemporary American culture. Thus for instance braiding of hair into elaborate coiffures referred to in 1 Timothy 2:9 and 1 Peter 3:3 was interpreted by some as plaiting even in simple pigtails and prohibited.

It is inadequate to describe their method as naive literalism. They enunciated distinct, eternal "principles" they understood to be "direct revelation" in text form.[2] They then attempted to set forth regulations that would be consistent with these principles, such as humility, obedience, compassion, truthfulness, modesty, and service of others before self. Nonconformity itself was called a principle. "Consistency" was a primary consideration in their discernment and application of specific texts. Many of the dress codes, for example, were attempts to be consistent with the current concepts of modesty. They were not read simply as literal commands from Scripture, although where Scripture prohibited specific practices they tried to literally follow.

Their application of nonconformity to evil in the world clearly follows the analogy of Israel's concept of holiness as separation from the nations around them (Lev. 18: 2-3). This analogy virtually erased the distance between ancient Israel and modern Mennonites and located them in biblical times. That being the case, they made the words of Jesus, "It has been said, . . . but I say to you." (Matt. 5:21ff) a hermeneutical shibboleth to deal with the many Old Testament commandments that did not fit their modern context. In this manner again the distance between themselves and the extreme ancient contextual situation was disposed of. The difference between themselves and the New Testament went unrecognized for all practical purposes.

This analogy seemed all the more obvious in America, where they were a minority German group in a predominantly English culture. Holiness meant separation from "worldliness"—meaning avoidance of cultural, political, and social activities of the surrounding society. The church was a cultural community with a distinct pattern of life defined in the "counsels and deliberations of conference" based on scriptural principles to which the nonconformed members were expected to be "loyal."[3] "English" practices, even religious and church practices, were studiously avoided.

The End of "Restrictions"

Now that holiness is no longer defined in the language of cultural separation, terms like "unequal yoke," purity, and restrictions are no longer part of common Mennonite community vocabulary. Restrictions on social, political, and commercial activities of the surrounding society no longer define the "pure" church. Now that loyalty to the church and obedience to biblical rules and principles as defined by its ordained leaders no longer mark out the "narrow way," what is the relevance of Scripture? How do we arrive at its meaning for today? How is the text of Scripture related to the Spirit that the Johnnine Jesus promised to send his followers to lead them into all truth?

Discernment has become a much-used word in church vocabulary, but what does it in fact include? How are we to discern the meaning of canonical texts that we consider normative for our life together? Are debate, dialogue, disputation, and discipline part of the process? What role do we allot to the Holy Spirit, and how is that role manifested in the life of the church? How shall we evaluate the significance of experience in the discernment process? These are by no means new questions, but they have become extremely relevant again in the life of the church.

How do we move from the first century (New Testament) to the twenty-first century to authentically apply the spiritual and moral wisdom of Scripture's pages? How does the acquisition of new knowledge affect the discernment process? Our understanding of the nature of the universe, of the causes of disease, of the relativity of cultural knowledge itself—all affect the way we read the Bible. How does the movement of history, which involves major cultural changes, affect it? As we attempt to apply "biblical," i.e., ancient conceptualizations, to contemporary moral categories, how do we determine that "*this is that* which was spoken by the prophet" as the first church did (Acts 2:16 KJV, emphasis added)?[4]

The distance between the New Testament and today is far greater than the distance between the two testaments! Does anyone really know the difference between 15 billion years and eternity? Can we really discriminate between "viruses" and "spirits," or the discrete difference between "psyche" and "soma" as the cause of sickness? How shall we distinguish the beginning of "human," i.e., spiritual-personal, life from the moment of physical fertilization of the ovum to the first cry of a newborn infant? Are the more primitive categories of the New Testament writings determinative in making these distinctions?

Some decades ago J. B. Phillips wrote a book entitled *Your God is Too Small* in which he gave examples of ways we still think of God in preindustrial and pretechnological terms—a God, for example, who does not understand the workings of current technology. In a real sense we are still facing that dilemma! How does God and "God's Word" relate to the great moral and social issues that face the church? Does a God of the prescientific and pre-technological universe demand that we interpret his (yes, the God of that universe was a male!) presence among us and will for us in terms that no longer really control our lives? How is God's Word, garbed in the text of ancient culture and language, to be discerned? What in the contemporary situation is analogous to the ancient reference? How can an ancient authoritative text relate to a current situation?

The question is crucial for the church, and especially so for its use of the New Testament. Apostolic doctrinal explanations are based on ancient metaphors and concepts. How, for example, does the mystical concept of atonement through blood sacrifice translate in a secular social order where blood is simply the fluid running through our veins carrying nourishment and oxygen to and wastes from our bodies? Their moral instruction is based on ancient cultural perceptions and values. How shall we contextualize its characterization of women's role in the church, its sexual and family advice that presupposes the authority of the husband-father-master over his wives, children, and slaves? The current claim, for example, that marriage (and therefore sexual privileges) has always been defined as one man and one woman is simply incorrect even for the Bible. Is it an eternal principle that has finally been recognized? How do Peter and Paul's political exhortations to "subjects" of the emperor, not "citizens" of the state, relate to a democratic order? How can the ideal of *Nachfolge Christi* (discipleship) apply in our contemporary professionalized and individualized social order?

I am well aware that on many of these issues we have arrived at intuited solutions that are given the benefit of the doubt in society, especially religious society. Indeed many of the inherited positions based on the Western rational tradition, natural law, evolving social mores, and authoritative textual interpretations virtually have the authority of the Bible itself. Traditional patterns of contextualization formed over time change very slowly, especially if they have the imprimatur of politically and socially established religion. It was precisely this kind of moral and religious inertia that the Anabaptists of the sixteenth century challenged. Although the issues themselves may have changed, the continuing challenge in the name of spiritual biblical discernment remains.

The Meaning of Scripture for Today

The "Word" of God is spoken in conversational form, and in a conversation the meaning of words is determined from both sides—the speaker's side and the hearer's side. In some sense it is true that what the speaker says, i.e., means, is what the hearer understands him/her to have said. This is an important point because the Word of God comes to us as a textual report in the Bible written in the languages and conventions of the ancient cultural world.

The fact that revelation is in a conversational form, which requires immediate perception and response from the ancients who first received it, accentuates the Bible's character as an ancient communication. In gracious condescension God "spoke" in the languages of the ancient hearers, not in a generic unidirectional verbal symbol that is unchanging for all time. This complicates the discovery of its "meaning" for our lives in the contemporary world, but consider the consequences if it had not been so! If God had tried to communicate in contemporary scientific thought forms and terminology, no one could have understood until the nineteenth or twentieth centuries! While we claim that the Bible is a word for today, and I certainly believe that, we have not majored in its contextualization.

Revelation in the Christian tradition has been understood as a historical communication in which God is the Teacher, but often the teacher has been assumed to be a lecturer. Most of our metaphors assume that revelation comes as an oracular, unidirectional pronouncement on morals and doctrine, as in the case of the Ten Commandments. The Speaker and the Speaker alone determines the meaning, and the hearer strains to understand and obey at her/his peril. God's grace is manifested in divine patience with our severe spiritual and rational handicap. Protestant Orthodoxy's emphasis on the transcendence of God and the depravity and limitation of human beings has tended to amplify this conception of revelation as eternal, immutable principles which are to be propagated across cultures in unaltered form.

But if we take our clue from John 1:1-14, this is not the case. The *Logos* (word, meaning) that through the ages shone as a light in the darkness now takes the form of cultural embodiment and converses with us. This Logos assumes local Jewish identity, adopting the local worldview, and speaking the local language. He lives in mutual dependence and interaction with his companions. His own self-understanding develops in interaction with them, and he expresses confidence that as they imbibe his Spirit they will be led into all truth (John 16:12-14).

By historical revelation we mean that God's Word comes to us not as an immutable transcultural, trans-historical pronouncement from beyond history, but as a personal word of enlightenment in our own situation, which involves us in decision about our next steps. As light it shines upon our own cultural landscape illuminating the path to life (John 8:12ff) and demanding our discriminating response (John 3:19ff). It is "God with us" speaking to us within the confines of our own cultural limitations (Matt. 1:23). Thus it comes to us in a cultural context, in a given time and place and language, which presupposes a particular limited perception and transmission. One simply can not escape this aspect of historical existence in crossing cultural borders, either historical or spatial, with revealed truth.

This conversational metaphor can also be applied to the relation of the biblical text to the cultural context in which it is being read. As the written record of revelation, its meaning is not contained wholly within itself but discloses itself in relation to the culture in which it is being read. In Stephen Fowl's terminology, there is no one "determined" meaning of the text that exists separate and apart from its cultural interpretations and applications.[5] The meaning of the text must be discerned in a dialogue with its cultural contexts. Note that we have said contexts (plural)—its ancient and its contemporary contexts, the contexts of its original writers and readers and of its present-day readers. Actually it is not quite that simple. We must take into account the writer's intended meaning, the original readers' perception of the text's meaning, then the meaning for readers in the changing cultural and language patterns over time down to the present. This latter reading is usually referred to as tradition.

It is the *import* of Scripture, not its literal original wording, that is to be contextualized. Replicating what was commanded in an ancient cultural situation may in fact contradict its original import. Scripture's import must take into account the *function* of the text in its original situation. For example, much of the instruction to Christian women in 1 Timothy is for the purpose of public relations ("so as to give the adversary no occasion to revile us" 5:14). And even exhortation concerning joining in pagan religious services, as well as eating non-kosher meat, is summed up under the rubric, "'All things are lawful' but not all things are beneficial" (1 Cor. 10:23).

The import of scriptural texts must make room for the Spirit's intent voiced through the author. It cannot be simply identified with the author's intent or the literal words of the text. The author's private intent may in fact not be obvious, or it may be limited through partial understanding of the Spirit's intent or the mitigating circumstances of those being addressed.[6] Here, for example, traditional social constructs, values, and patterns that regulated the status of slaves and marital-family relationships, and defined the meaning of physical sexual relations obviously influenced and limited the exhortations of the apostolic writers. Not only the social context and worldview of the immediate receptors, but the ongoing changing cultural patterns (which in some cases were brought about by the initial teaching of those who interpreted the original text) must be considered. Thus to speak of the "import" of Scripture is to speak of more than a descriptive exegesis of the original text as intended and perceived in the first instance.[7] This calls for discriminating discernment of both the original situation and text and the contemporary context into which it is being translated and applied.

Without going into the technicalities of the hermeneutical process, this implies, as indeed historical interpretations and cultural applications demonstrate, that the meaning of any given scriptural instruction, moral or doctrinal, may and will vary over time as cultures and languages vary. The contemporary import or meaning of a biblical dictate may not be expressed in precisely the same terms or actions as the original requires. Indeed, to authentically perpetuate the original import of Scripture one may, as James Brenneman points out in his reflections on

Deuteronomy, need to disobey the actual biblical command, as for example, the command to stone rebellious children.[8]

Using Scripture in the Church Today

There are, of course, many legitimate and profitable personal uses of Scripture in our context. Scripture may be used as a spiritual guide for meditation and inspiration or as a theological or ethical guide to stir and challenge the imagination. It may legitimately be used as an intellectual tool in historical or geographical investigation although this is not strictly a religious use.

Here, however, we are not concerned with these personal ad hoc uses. The Bible is "the book of the church," as David Kelsey points out,[9] and its primary intended use is to enlighten and guide the life and decisions of the church. The church recognized the "inspired" character of the Bible and has defined the canon of books it considers normative for its ongoing life and mission. It submits itself to the Bible as Scripture—the authoritative, inspired Word of God. In the best of all possible worlds, understanding and applying its normative message should be a simple process, but as the great variety of both doctrine and practical ethics in the churches indicates, the process is far from simple.

In a word, the complication with using the Bible as a normative directive today lies in its character as a *historical* revelation. If it were in fact a "direct revelation" of infallible transcultural truths, as Mennonite leaders of the past generation viewed it, our task in crossing cultures would still be difficult but considerably simplified. As it is, the Bible is a record and witness to a revelation given over several millennia. The Bible itself became an agent of change and as history progressed altered the cultural context in which it was given.[10] Its perspectives, social functions, religious and moral regulations change as it effects changes in the cultures to which it comes. Prior revelation is continually being recontextualized in the Bible itself as the social and cultural context changes.

One can illustrate this from the changes in our own Western christianized culture. Many of the significant cultural changes of the past century are at least in part the effects of biblical revelation. Changes in the social status of women, the essential meaning and function of marriage, the role of sexual relationships, the abolition of slavery, the recognition of human equality of all ethnic and racial groups—all require a different reading of the Scriptures than in preceding centuries. As the conversation progresses and the context changes, the meaning of texts is construed differently.

Perhaps an illustration of how changes in the fields of science and technology have affected our reading of the Bible will help clarify the point. Considerable portions of Scripture were written during the Ptolemaic era and presuppose an outdated conception of the universe—a flat earth with Jerusalem at its center and the heavenly spheres overarching it. God's home is just beyond the heavens in which the sun and moon move across the sky at the will of divine beings. Biblical language, metaphors, and allusions all reflect this concept.

Although we still use the language of a four-cornered earth and the sun rising in the east and going down in the west, we read it as poetic imagery, not empirical fact. We make this adjustment in reading almost without thought and probably write off the Flat Earth Society as antiquarian. But this reconceptualization has profound implications for our concept of God's relation to us. And it is our contention here that if the Bible is to be useful to us as normative Scripture in today's world, the church needs to self-consciously make these kinds of cultural adaptations in its reading and application of biblical texts.

This need to make cultural adaptations in translating the meaning (reading) of the text is made still more complicated by the culture-crossing mission of the church. Indeed, the command of Jesus to go into the world and teach all nations to become his disciples (Matt. 28:20) raises the questions of cultural translation and contextualization far more intensely than does the intellectual hermeneutics of postmodernism. The authentic import of the gospel message must be "translated" into and applied in each different cultural situation. It is one thing to translate a universal unchanging principle into the language of differing cultures. It is quite another to identify with and embody the message of the gospel in each of these differing cultures.

One contemporary example of this difficulty of cultural translation and contextualization of the text is being played out at in the ongoing debate about sexuality in the worldwide Anglican Communion. Bishops from traditional patriarchally oriented societies with their views of male-female relations, the nature of the family, and the role of sex have threatened to leave the Communion because some bishops from a Western society have ordained a gay bishop in a situation that is no longer "traditional." If the original biblical taboo recorded in Leviticus 18 against same-sex genital activity is understood as an eternal universal principle to be proclaimed and put into effect wherever Christianity is preached, its application whether in the Unites States or Africa is relatively straightforward. If the taboo is a culturally conditioned restriction to be understood within tribalistic Hebrew and Jewish society, then its cross-cultural adaptation and implementation must be more nuanced. Given the diachronic nature of cultural phenomena—that is, their continuously changing character over a period of time—this kind of tension is bound to exist within as well as between cultures.

This process of translation and application, as Luke Timothy Johnston and others have pointed out, is not merely one of making the intellectual distinction between an ancient worldview and the modern one, or between a descriptive biblical theology and a functioning theological translation in contemporary idiom. The process does, of course, assume the need to distinguish what Krister Stendahl has called "the two tenses" of meaning—"What *did* it mean?" and "What *does* it mean?" [11] It involves spiritual and moral discernment that recognizes the authority of Scripture and captures its import in an authentic modern transition of meaning and practice. Involved is what Johnson calls "the complex task of negotiating normative texts and continuing human experiences."[12]

From a theological perspective, I suggest that this will involve three things: first, a new recognition of the dynamic role of the Holy Spirit in the life of the church; second, a renewed focus on Jesus Christ as the "pioneer and perfecter of our faith" (Heb. 12:2) rather than admonitory texts; and third, an ethic of discipleship as apprenticeship rather than "restrictions" of nonconformity.

The Spirit is directly related to the experience of the church in its ongoing process of embodying the genuine message and spirit of Christ in human cultures. (This process is sometimes called inculturation.) As the life breath of the body of Christ representing the true message of Jesus, the Spirit is the moral dynamic and discriminating guide of the church. The essentially new identity of the Spirit disclosed in the New Testament is precisely this: that the Spirit is the Spirit of Jesus of Nazareth. This is the heart of the Johnnine Christ's comforting promise to his followers just before his death (John 14–16).

In the Anabaptist Mennonite tradition as well as the Reformed tradition from which it stems, the Holy Spirit's role has been carefully circumscribed by Scripture. We have always been assured that the Spirit would never reveal anything contrary to the text of Scripture.

Technically this may be true when properly explained. However, it has usually served to buttress and sustain the conventional interpretation of the text. In seeking to protect itself from traditional Roman Catholicism's melding of the Holy Spirit and Holy Office on the one hand and the vagaries of spiritualism and charismatic Pentecostalism on the other, the Mennonite tradition has virtually made the Spirit subservient to the text of Scripture. This tendency has been intensified by the impact of modern Fundamentalism, which puts emphasis on the infallible text. Although it admits that the Spirit is the authoritative source of Scripture, it has defined the Spirit's revelatory role as subservient and limited in time to the apostolic period.[13]

According to John's Gospel, the Spirit is the new presence of Jesus himself with his followers (14:28). It comes as the *Parakletos* (Paraclete), one called to their side as enabler and guide, defining the true nature of the world, discriminating between the idiosyncrasies of culture and unbelief (16: 8-11). Throughout the changing temporal context, the Spirit plays an interlocutive role with the text in the church's ongoing cultural assimilation. The text in this case presents the literal culture-bound example of the historical Jesus, and the Spirit directs the discerning representation, or cultural translation, of the original.

It is precisely the Spirit that frees the church to cross-cultural boundaries with an authentic contextualization of the historical record, i.e., the text. This applies, of course, not only to the boundaries of changing historical norms but also to the geographical variations of cultural norms and practice.

This coming of the Spirit/Parakletos, Jesus says, will be an "advantage" to the disciples (16:7); he encourages them to go forth in confidence. This advantage has been variously understood in relation to the text of Scripture. In verse 13 it is described as "guiding [them] into all the truth," which Jesus in his historical role had not been able to do. Is this advantage in the giving of an inspired text in contrast to an oral tradition? Is it in the revelation of new esoteric prophetic knowledge, which Jesus could not impart within the limits of his historical mission? Is the advantage in the Spirit's enabling role (sanctification)? Is it to be found in the mode of spiritual intuition guiding the disciples in shifting, conflictual settings?

All of these are significant questions, but from a hermeneutical perspective the relation of text and Spirit takes precedence. I would argue that the advantage does not refer to a text inspired by the Spirit in contrast to an oral tradition, although for historical accuracy there are clear advantages to be had in an inspired canonical text. It is rather the advantage of a spiritual mode of presence over a textual mode of presence in the church. Inspiring a temporal text that gives direct literal doctrinal and ethical information did not fulfill the "guiding into all the truth." Such a truth statement would be culturally bound in the same way that the literal historical presence of Jesus in Palestine would have been. Human culture itself is dynamic, and increased knowledge of the world changes our self-understanding and our understanding of God's relation to the world.

The inspired text is, indeed, a next step in the ongoing role of the Spirit of Jesus in the church, and the church's canonization of the text recognizing its inspired normative character as the apostolic witness confirms this. But the Spirit's inspiration of the apostolic church to produce a record and witness is not the end of the Spirit's role in "guiding [the church] *into all the truth*." That role continues in the Spirit's continuing direction of the discerning hermeneutical use of the text by the church. Inspiration is not a special quality inherent in the written words of the Bible. The Bible is inspired if and when we allow the Spirit to communicate the authentic mind of Christ through its words.[14] Insofar, then, as the church interprets and applies the text according to the Spirit of Christ in the contemporary cultural situation, it functions as the inspired Word of God.

The second necessary hermeneutical adjustment involves a renewed focus on Jesus Christ as the "pioneer and perfecter of our faith" (Heb. 12:2) rather than admonitory texts such as the Sermon on the Mount and Romans 12–13. American Mennonite reading of the New Testament in the last century majored in the hortatory and regulatory passages. Focus was on Jesus as a Teacher/Rabbi and on "following" as obedience to instructions; on "Torah," which means divine guidance, as legal code rather than covenant relationship. It did not emphasize the spiritual dynamic of Jesus as exemplar—his relationship to God as "Abba," his compassion for the impoverished and wayward, his forgiving love for sinners, his healing power for the suffering, and his passion for peacemaking.

The promise of John 16:14 is that the Holy Spirit will "glorify" Jesus—put the spotlight on him and expand on what he has begun. The Holy Spirit, as we have already noted, is not a third and new revelation of God but is the extension of the presence and activity of Jesus as the Messiah. Thus the focus and emphasis remains on Jesus, not simply as a new lawgiver like Moses or a better atoning cultic sacrifice, but as "the true and living Way" to God (John 14:6). The Spirit reveals the "mind of Christ," and as the go-between entitles and empowers Jesus' followers to share in his life and continue his mission.

Finally, such a refocusing on Jesus as the divine exemplar requires a new emphasis on the meaning of following Jesus. It is not intended to, nor will it, diminish the substantive meaning of discipleship. Rather it shifts the focus from "restrictions" to transformation. It highlights the relationship of the disciple as apprentice to the master. The aim of an apprentice is not rote copying but mastery of the art or craft in the spirit of the master (Phil. 3:12). The technique of apprenticeship is authentic imitation, so that one's works evidence the hallmark of the master craftsman.[15]

Discerning the Authentic Import of Scripture

The theological analysis and hermeneutic that I have offered presents a rationale for the church as a hermeneutical community, but this raises many unresolved practical questions of implementation and expectation. Indeed, although the word *discernment* has become a kind of icon for the believers church ideal, little practical attention has been given to its meaning and process.[16] While the scope of this chapter does not allow extended consideration of these questions, some attention to the nature and expected results of the discernment process are indicated in closing.

In the "free church" tradition we seem to have arrived at the point where "free" means free to leave denominational groupings. Like divorce, schism has become an acceptable way to resolve differences in understandings and values in the church community! For many, to be free means to be "independent" and to interpret sectarian separation as a sign of faithfulness. Or in the case of individuals, freedom means the right to move from congregation to congregation and from denomination to denomination until commonality is found. This no doubt reflects the heightened individualism of our age, but it also may be in part the result of failure to find a workable model of congregational discernment. Denominational structuring and leadership models of the past century are defunct, and new models have not replaced them.

Discernment in the biblical sense is a group process under the tutelage of the Holy Spirit. Without giving a full biblical rationale, we may cite the process of the apostolic church as it resolved the question of circumcision and full Gentile participation in its life (Acts 10-15) as a model. According to the Corinthian epistles, discernment involves a congregational process of evaluating apostolic advice and prophetic insight, with due deference being given to apostolic authority. Discernment was not a "right" of individual conscience, and the only option for those who did not submit to the congregation's decisions seems to have been appropriate discipline of individuals.

Before we can seriously work with the process, however, several questions must be resolved. What is the locus of the process? Who is qualified to make decisions normative for the congregation? What outcome do we expect from the process? And what are the agreed-upon norms which the group would reference in making a decision?

In the past century, the various Mennonite denominations have differed slightly in their polity of congregational autonomy, but by and large discernment and decision-making has been left in the hands of representative leadership at the district and national conference levels. These committees were made up of clergy, informed laity (presumably recognizing congregational participation), and scholars usually from one of the seminaries or colleges. Issues of cultural and moral sensitivity, largely in the realm of ethics rather than doctrine, might be assigned for ongoing study and recommendation to national and district denominational conference committees. Such committees might function as "continuing communities," e.g., "The Peace Problems Committee" of the (Old) Mennonite Church, and assemble special study conferences. Ultimately decisions were reported to the congregations, which may or may not have been included in the earlier processes, as the teaching and recommendation of the church for their consideration.

While the deliberation process certainly took congregational life and opinion into account, the congregations did not function as a discernment group sharing directly in the process. Individual laity might enter their opinions to the larger church through letters to the editors of church publications, but it has not been clear what role this debating and disputing plays in the discernment process. It rather obviously does not represent congregational decision-making. In any case, it seldom if ever represents the considered position arrived at by congregational discernment. Thus it certainly does not represent the teaching and pastoral office of the local congregation.

In short, up to the present the local congregation has not been considered the locus for discernment. Local teaching and pastoral ministries have not been oriented this way. How the changes in local church life and organization, which are represented in the changed role of the pastor, should be reflected in the discernment process remains a question.

The second question we must agree upon is our expectations of the process. The religious, social, and political influences that impact our congregations have created a very different congregational climate. The degree of uniformity in life and thought that characterized an earlier period no longer exists. When we add to this the great diversity of cultures which now characterize the present Mennonite World Conference, we cannot expect the uniformity of thought and practice that was so greatly valued by an earlier generation to result from discernment.

This brings us to the question of what norm or norms are to be brought to the discernment process. Divergent and changing views about the Bible itself still cause considerable tension in the church and account for many disagreements on how to read it in the present situation. While we acknowledge the authority of the Bible, how shall we interpret and apply that authority when making decisions in our contemporary world? The believers church has not given formal recognition to tradition—the accumulation over time of authoritative interpretations—as a norm. Nevertheless tradition has played a considerable role in interpretation and decision-making. In changing times, how are we to recognize the voice of the Spirit in the experience of the church when it speaks in unconventional or non-traditional terms? How do we get from the meaning of Scripture "then" to its meaning "now" in vastly different circumstances? Until we have resolved these difficulties, we can not expect to make much progress in the discernment process.

In concluding, then, I suggest four requisites for successful discernment. These are not procedural but presuppositional requisites.

First, we will need to agree on what the authority of the Bible as record and witness to revelation implies for its use in contemporary cultures. How do we honor the authentic import of the original text without being bound by it as a procrustean document to be literally replicated? This, as noted earlier, will involve a more careful consideration of the role of the Holy Spirit's dynamic relation to the text.

Second, we will need to genuinely value the ideal reality of the church as the sacramental community and "body of Christ." The "believers church" is not the believers' church: it does not belong to the members in the fashion of a Lockean[17] society. Recognition of the church as Christ's body implies willingness within the limits of conscience to submit one's own judgment to the judgment of the group.

Third, we must be willing to give more careful and objective attention to the evaluation of changes in our contemporary culture. In his summary of a study by Stephen Farris, Joel Green has stated it well. "Coherence requires both similarity to the biblical witness and dissimilarity, the latter arising from our attending to the passage of time and the changes that accompany it since a biblical text first served as a particular, concrete word from God. *What is required, then, is exegesis of one's own world set in relation to exegesis of the biblical text, so that one can move from text to proclamation*" (italics mine).[18] We have majored in biblical exegesis but have done little to critically evaluate both the good and the bad in contemporary society.

We must be open to unconventional promptings and insights of the Spirit in the experience of the church as it maneuvers the transitions from culture to culture in both history and geographical location. As Loveday Alexander says so well in her essay, "'This is That:' The Authority of Scripture in the Acts of the Apostles,"

> How did we get into the trap of treating the Bible as a frozen text? And, more to the point, how can we get out of it? Can we find resources in the Bible itself for a biblical approach to scriptural authority that avoids the dilemma of the frozen mammoth? This is, I believe, one of the most vital theological tasks facing us in the church today. . . .[19]

Alexander's essay shows how the church allowed the Spirit to direct the use of Scripture in ways a literal interpretation may never have suggested! The reverse of this is to let the text restrict the movement of the Spirit.

Finally, we must find a formula of discernment[20] that will allow us to continue *dialogue-in-fellowship* where sincere divergence in understandings, interpretations, and applications of Scripture persist—a unity without uniformity. This is a polity issue as well as a hermeneutical one. Perhaps we have arrived at the place where what defines unity is agreement on the fundamental questions that deserve discernment rather than the uniformity of the answers that the process might arrive at. Here, for example, questions of nonviolence and the proper limits of participation in secular political society still define the parameters of Mennonite communions.[21] Up to the present, Mennonite conferences have found it easier to deal with this kind of cultural divergence in their cross-cultural missions than among themselves on the home turf. The Mennonite World Conference movement gives witness to this and may provide the pattern of how to proceed in the future.

Notes

1. In his 1929 edition of *Doctrines of the Bible*, a revision of the earlier 1914 version, Kauffman used but disavowed the terminology of restrictions. In chapter 6 he wrote, "With this subject we begin the study of a number of scriptural teachings commonly known as 'restrictions.' They are *restrictions* to the extent that they serve as a warning and a restraining power, but they may more properly be called *Gospel principles* for those whose lives are governed by the Word of God." (Scottdale, Pa.: Mennonite Publishing House, 1929)

2. In the 1929 edition of *Doctrines of the Bible,* Kauffman referred to "principles of everlasting truth" (p. 135) and "direct revelation" in the Bible (p. 141). J. B. Smith, who wrote the original article on the Bible in the 1914 edition upon which Kauffman's version is based, had used the same kind of language. Smith's chapter shows clear influence of the Bible Conference Movement, which self-consciously rebutted the "Liberalism" of the day that preceded the Fundamentalism of the 1920s and 1930s; see my *Dispensationalism in America: Its Rise and Development* (Richmond, Va.: John Knox, 1958.) In this respect Kauffman's language indicates a fundamentalist language and concern that was not present in his 1898 *Manuel of Bible Doctrines*. Indeed, there is no chapter on the Bible in that edition.

3. *Bible Doctrine: A Treatise on the Great Doctrines of the Bible,* Compiled by a committee appointed by Mennonite General Conference, Daniel Kauffman, editor (Scottdale, Pa.: Mennonite Publishing House, 1914), 525-26. The context for this interpretation is succinctly stated on the previous page. "God has provided His Church with regulations which help each honest soul to keep pure and continue to press onward as a light-bearer. The first essential to a well disciplined church is that applicants for membership are fully surrendered to God, willing to submit themselves as instruments of righteousness unto God. When the church is lax in presenting the whole counsel of God, and opens her doors to those who bring with them the marks of this world and its spirit, it can never hope to make itself a fold of protection to guard its lambs from evil."

4. In an insightful essay entitled "'This is That': The Authority of Scripture in the Acts of the Apostles" Loveday Alexander, Professor of Biblical Studies at the University of Sheffield, discusses the way in which the New Testament Church itself made use of Scripture that points the way to contemporary usage; *The Princeton Seminary Bulletin*, 25.2 (2004): 188-204.

5. Stephen E. Fowl, *Engaging Scripture: A Model for Theological Interpretation* (Malden, Mass.: Blackwell, 1998), 32-40.

6. Paul clearly establishes this principle when he distinguishes between his own judgment and that of "the Lord," (1 Cor. 7:12) and when he exhorts the Corinthians to imitate him as he imitates Christ (1 Cor. 11:1). Peter also implies this when he exhorts his readers to "follow in his [Christ's] steps" rather than his own (1 Peter 2:21).

7. In his chapter, "Tradition, Authority, and a Christian Approach to the Bible as Scripture," Trevor Hart writes, "Furthermore, the answers given in one social or cultural context will not, in and of themselves, be likely to serve other contexts especially well, and must be reforged as the question of meaning is asked ever afresh in the church's constant return to the text of Scripture. There is a diachronic and a synchronic dimension to this sense in which the text of Scripture will always 'mean' something slightly different, depending where, when, and for what purpose we interrogate or seek to hear it. This is not to suggest that particular communities may do with or make of the text what they like, so that in theory radically different or contradictory answers could easily be entertained"; *Between Two Horizons: Spanning New Testament Studies and Systematic Theology*, ed. Joel B. Green and Max Turner (Grand Rapids: Eerdmans, 2000), 190)

8. *On Jordan's Stormy Banks: Lessons from the Book of Deuteronomy* (Scottdale, Pa.: Herald Press, 2004), 75ff.

9. David H. Kelsey, *The Uses of Scripture in Recent Theology* (Philadelphia: Fortress, 1975), see especially chapter 5, "Scripture."

10. See Trevor Hart's diagram and explanation in *Between Two Horizons*, 191.

11. "Biblical Theology, Contemporary," *The Interpreter's Dictionary of the Bible*," vol. 1, (Nashville: Abingdon Press, 1962), 418-432.

12. See "Debate and Discernment, Scripture and the Spirit," in *Virtues and Practices in the Christian Tradition*, ed. Nancey Murphy, Brad J. Kallenberg and Mark Thiessen Nation (Harrisburg, Pennsylvania: Trinity Press, 1997), 215ff. Johnson adds, "Within the faith community, this means an openness to the ways in which God's revelation continues in human experience as well as a deep commitment to the conviction that such revelation, while often, at first, perceived as dissonant with the symbols of Scripture, will, by God's grace directing human fidelity, be seen as consonant with those symbols and God's own fidelity. Essentially, however, the call of faith is to the living God whose revelation continues, rather than to *our previous understanding of the texts.*"

For a fuller treatment of the subject see Luke Timothy Johnson, *Scripture and Discernment: Decision Making in the Church* (Nashville: Abingdon Press), 1996.

13. Although B. B. Warfield, the early twentieth-century spokesperson for orthodox Reformed theology, calls the Spirit "the executive of the Godhead" in both Testaments, he defines the Spirit's role of inspiration in "the process of God's self-revelation" as an assigned, not an initiatory one. And in his definition of infallible verbal-plenary

inspiration he virtually limits the Spirit further disclosures to the inspired text. The Spirit "leads" believers according to the revelation given in the text, but no longer reveals. Of course, he might argue that the doctrine of the Trinity makes this kind of analytical distinction improper, nevertheless in actual ecclesial practice he firmly ruled out the possibility of any further disclosure in the experience of the church. See "The Spirit of God in the Old Testament," 127-156, and "The Leading of the Spirit," 543-559, in B. B. Warfield, *Biblical and Theological Studies*, ed. Samuel Craig (Philadelphia: Presbyterian and Reformed Publishing Company, 1952).

14. This should not be interpreted to mean that "the Bible *contains* the word of God," or that some parts are more inspired than others. It is merely to recognize that inspiration is not reified in the text, but is the continuing influence of the Spirit in relation to the text. That interpretation which represents the genuine spirit/breath of Jesus in the contemporary situation is the "inspired" word of God for that situation.

15. For further definition of discipleship to Jesus see my *God Our Savior: Theology in a Christological Mode* (Scottdale, Pa.: Herald Press, 1991), 39-40.

16. Ironically, one of the best works on the subject has been done by a Roman Catholic scholar, Luke Timothy Johnson, and is published by a Methodist press. See *Scripture and Discernment: Decision Making in the Church* (Abingdon Press, 1983). See also other references in this essay.

17. The English philosopher John Locke (1632-1704) is the acknowledged father of contemporary democratic individualism.

18. *Between Two Horizons*, p. 39.

19. The *Princeton Seminary Bulletin* 25.2 (2004): 190. The "dilemma of the frozen animal" metaphor comes from an archeological discovery of a mammoth found frozen solid in a glacier. To leave the animal frozen results in not examining the closely. Removing it means its slow but inevitable decay. "We seem to be faced with a stark choice (often made all the starker by the polarities of polemic) between a conservative ethic that takes the biblical text at face value as the truth revealed once and for all in the past, and a more liberal ethic, which appears to undermine (or ignore) the authoritative status of the Bible," p. 189.

20. For example, perhaps the phrase "teaching position of the church" that seems to be coming into formal use offers an approach to dealing with a variety of applications and practices in local congregations.

21. Such concerns, for example, clearly distinguish Mennonites from more right wing, socially assimilated Christian groups like our Southern Baptist friends.

2

Anabaptist or Mennonite? Interpreting the Bible

How and why have Mennonites around the world begun to use the term *Anabaptist* to describe their church position? Are Mennonites Anabaptists by virtue of being Mennonite? If not, what is the difference? Are only Mennonites Anabaptists? What about the other believers who belong to "free," or "believers' churches"? For example, should the Baptist denominations in America be included as Anabaptists? If not, what differences would exclude them? The late James McClendon, who grew up in the Baptist tradition, used the lower case "b" to include all those who shared a theology of voluntary church and discipleship. This seems to suggest that "anabaptism" and "believers church" are synonymous. Is there a generic anabaptism—"anabaptist" with a lower case "a"—and if so, what does it mean?

This essay suggests that the original Anabaptists were neither biblical literalists nor sectarians; and that generic anabaptism should not be understood as a new orthodoxy but rather as an authentic perspective on reading Scripture.

THE PROBLEM OF PLURALISTIC INTERPRETATIONS

Virtually every denomination or theological grouping has its own set of commentaries—Baptist, Methodist, Presbyterian (Reformed), Lutheran, Ecumenical, Evangelical, Catholic, Believers Church (Mennonite/Church of the Brethren), liberal, conservative, fundamentalist. How much of this is due to ecclesiastical conviction and concern, and how much to publishing companies' entrepreneurial enterprise may be in question! However, this raises a set of related questions. What is implied when we speak of "perspectives" in biblical interpretation? The Bible is read and interpreted from many perspectives, both Jewish and Christian. Is only one of these perspectives correct? Is there only one orthodox interpretation of each biblical text? Missionaries of previous centuries assumed that there was.

Biblical scholars of different religious traditions can pretty well agree on the historical contexts—language, culture, situational background—of the texts, and on the contemporary meaning of the words, at least on their ambiguity. The *Anchor Bible* commentaries written by Jewish, Catholic, and Protestant scholars were planned to interpret the Scriptures from this historical perspective. But the more difficult question is their significance for present-day multicultural contexts.

Should we be content with pluralistic interpretations of Scripture? Should we expect the Bible to have many different meanings and interpretations for different people? Is its message primarily for personal inspiration, instruction, and encouragement? Are its texts read more or less at random intended to serendipitously meet the need of the moment? Or do they primarily speak to larger theological and social issues that define the unity of the ecumenical church? If so, how do we go about understanding their correct meaning and application? What is the significance of an *anabaptist perspective*?

Whose responsibility is it to unpack and apply the biblical message? Is it scholars, priests, preachers, or officially appointed church study committees? Is it primarily the responsibility of each congregation and its leadership? Or is it "everyone for him- or herself?" If we talk about an anabaptist perspective, are we suggesting that this is the only correct perspective? Or are we proposing it as a conversational position to be considered in the larger, ecumenical discussion of the Bible? Although we cannot speak to all of these questions in a brief essay, all of these issues are implied in our recognition of anabaptist perspectives.

Current Meaning of "Anabaptist" in Mennonite Circles

At the turn of the twentieth century there was a generally recognized American "Mennonite perspective" on the meaning and application of Scripture. Common ethnic mores considered consistent with biblical ethics characterized Mennonite communities. Social and economic patterns inherited from Europe were adapted to meet the conditions of the American frontier and handed down in a tradition of biblical interpretation. These behavior patterns were preached from the pulpit in a recognized style of exposition.

Then at the turn of the century this German Mennonite tradition collided with the emerging Fundamentalist movement, a movement of predominantly English origin and closely linked to the King James Version, that was making exclusive claims to correct (orthodox) biblical interpretation. In its battle with "Liberalism" and higher criticism of the Bible, Fundamentalism insisted on literalistic precision in interpretation of Scripture as God's very words of instruction to humankind.

The impact of this fundamentalistic literalism on Mennonites who until then had assumed that they were literally following the biblical teachings led to a sea-change in Mennonite biblical interpretation, application, and preaching style. Mennonite pulpits began to apply fundamentalist literalism to New Testament teachings on dress, adornment with gold, use of alcohol and tobacco, sexual mores, the "spiritual" life, evangelistic outreach and missions, and what they dubbed "restrictions" demanded by the nonconformed life. For example, John S. Coffman introduced a literalistic interpretation of 1 Corinthians 11:1-17 that eventually made the wearing of a prayer covering a biblical requirement for Mennonite women.[1]

"Expository preaching," i.e., explaining a particular scriptural passage, became the model for sermons. The preacher did not simply choose a "text" of a verse or two to launch his own inspirational comments. Rather, guided by the church community tradition, he chose significant passages that could be expounded to support and encourage uniformity of belief and practice. At the climax of this style in the 1960s and 1970s, John R. Mumaw tried to give this approach some guidance with a book on expository preaching, but that came at the end of a long tradition and the beginning of a new hermeneutical approach.[2]

To understand the significance of an anabaptist perspective in contrast to a more general free church perspective on biblical interpretation, one needs to see its relation to this sectarian Mennonite perspective. What led the American Mennonites to renew their interest in their Anabaptist origins? Through the eighteenth and nineteenth centuries, they had continued to show interest in *Martyrs Mirror* and in the works of Menno Simons. But around the turn of the twentieth century, at the same time some of their leaders began to be acquainted with Moody and the fundamentalist revival movement, there was renewed interest in Anabaptism. The revivalist movement sparked new life and emphases into the old Mennonite patterns that raised questions about the source and validity of the contemporary American Mennonite tradition. This in turn raised the question of their Mennonite origins in the Anabaptist movement.

As Mennonite leaders came into contact with the dynamic revival movement, they became more self-consciously aware of themselves as a potentially competitive evangelical group. This in turn led them to explore their Anabaptist origins for precedents that could define their own distinctive character over against non-Anabaptist expressions of piety and mission. Men like Bishop John F. Funk, John S. Coffman, Menno Steiner, and other self-aware leaders who introduced a more dynamic and evangelistic strain of piety into the Mennonite communities looked to the sixteenth century for a model that could be followed in nineteenth- and twentieth-century America.

The first instinct was to identify Anabaptism and the essence of Mennonitism in contrasting it to Protestantism. In his *Mennonite History,* first written and published in 1927, Daniel Kauffman wrote, "When we say 'Mennonitism' we mean the same as Anabaptism, for the Mennonites (though not known by that name until later) were the pioneer Anabaptists."[3] He distinguished them from the Reformers as "nonresistant in life, and scripturally orthodox in fundamentalism" [sic]. The issue that divided them, he said, was twofold, namely " (1) State-Churchism [sic] Vs. individual conscience and choice; (2) the sword, and what is behind it." And he added, "While times have changed, circumstances now are different from what they were then, and issues have shifted somewhat, yet the fundamental difference between these two schools of thought and classes of people remains substantially the same."[4]

Skipping hurriedly over the years, in mid-century C. Henry Smith published his *Story of the Mennonites* (c. 1941) in which he portrayed Anabaptists as "the extreme Left [sic] of that day," and the origin of the conviction that "religion is a matter of individual conscience."[5] The next year (1942) John Horsch, who had been researching and writing on

Mennonite history, published his *Mennonites in Europe*. In it he portrayed Anabaptists as strict biblicists of high moral character and evangelistic zeal.[6] In a series of articles in *The Gospel Herald* earlier in the century he maintained that they were essentially a fundamentalistic movement of the Reformation.

In his *Conrad Grebel 1498-1526, Founder of the Swiss Brethren* (written earlier but published in 1950) Horsch's son-in-law, Harold Bender, portrayed "evangelical" Anabaptism as a biblically based New Testament movement with emphasis on "full Christian discipleship in its transformation of life after the pattern of Christ."[7] In his now famous presidential address to the American Church History Society in 1943, "The Anabaptist Vision," he spelled out the implications of this discipleship. It included a voluntary community of committed members, dedicated to the Scripture as the Word of God and the sole standard for the church, and committed to a life of nonresistant love. This Anabaptist perspective was identified and promoted as the ideal for the twentieth-century Mennonite denomination.

In the 1950s and early 1960s, church leaders in Pennsylvania and Virginia challenged this appeal to Anabaptist beliefs as an authoritative perspective for Mennonites today. They insisted that the first-century Bible, not the sixteenth-century Anabaptist interpretations, was the only authority.[8] By "Bible," however, they were defending certain doctrines such as premillennialism, inerrancy of the Bible, the "two-kingdom" theory of church and state, the necessity of a personal experience of salvation—all of which were current fundamentalist doctrines. They were afraid of an incipient "liberalism" and social emphasis on the gospel. They accepted John Horsch's fundamentalistic interpretation of Anabaptism, and they were suspicious of H. S. Bender and Guy F. Hershberger, who were propounding the new vision.

At the same time, there was growing dissatisfaction with the fundamentalist view of the biblical text. A more literary and experiential interpretation of the biblical text was being introduced into Mennonite circles through the "inductive approach" to biblical interpretation.[9] This new conservative but non-fundamentalistic perspective on the Bible is clearly reflected in the 1963 *Mennonite Confession of Faith*. Under the guiding hand of John C. Wenger, the language of the confession took on a more biblical character, signaling a distinct cultural shift away from a literalistic and sectarian understanding and application of Scripture.

This is epitomized in the self-conscious replacement of the phrase, "inerrant in its original writings" with "infallible Guide to lead men [sic] to faith in Christ." (Article 2)[10]

The *Confession of Faith in a Mennonite Perspective* (1995), drawn up by the two Mennonite groups, General Conference Mennonites and (Old) Mennonites that now form the Mennonite Church USA, continues this conservative but not fundamentalist approach to Scripture. It emphasizes the central hermeneutical importance of Christ for understanding the whole Bible, the authority of Scripture for the guidance of ethical behavior and the relation of the church to society, and the centrality of the congregation in discerning and testing biblical interpretation. (Article IV, p. 24) These clearly reflect what was then currently understood as distinctive "anabaptist" characteristics.

Impact of Transcultural Missions

The closing decades of the twentieth century saw a realignment of Mennonite loyalties. Significant groups, some in the name of "evangelical Anabaptism," some reacting against identification of anabaptist Mennonitism with peace and social service emphases, broke clear of the major Mennonite denominations. Cooperative projects, such as publishing Sunday school materials and a new hymnal-worship book, were undertaken by two major Mennonite groups and the Church of the Brethren. There was increasing cooperation between the various Mennonite-related groups on the mission field. All of these collaborative projects ignored twentieth-century differences in theology and practice and implied a common faith without clearly formulating its content. The 1995 Mennonite *Confession of Faith*, mentioned above, explicitly attempted to formulate a statement for the two largest Mennonite groups, who were in the process of merging, that "follows some traditional patterns, but also introduces new elements in line with their Anabaptist heritage."[11]

Beginning in the late 1970s, Mennonite denominational publisher Herald Press began planning for a Believers Church Bible Commentary Series, and the first volume came out in 1986. Mennonites, Brethren in Christ, Church of the Brethren, and the Mennonite Brethren sponsored the ongoing project. Use of the term *believers church* and the inclusion of a number of related groups indicate that they were seeking a more ecumenical perspective than the older name "Mennonite" implied, but the denominations included in the project all represent an anabaptist orientation. The Herald Press catalog does not explicitly advertise the series as Anabaptist, but it does emphasize that it is organized and written for "lay leaders" as well as teachers and pastors—clearly an anabaptist perspective. This shift in nomenclature indicates that the progressive groups were moving toward a more inclusive position as the attrition of conservative groups, who still felt more comfortable with the old Mennonite label, continued.

During this same post-World War II period, the Mennonite label began to feel restrictive on the mission field, but what was the alternative? Some Mennonite missionaries in Asia allied themselves with the fundamentalist evangelicalism, which emphasized personal conversion and church planting. Others were still convinced that the Mennonite tradition had something to offer to the evangelical Protestant world, even though they were abandoning the older literalistic traditions. Yet others began to stress an "incarnational" approach to witness and the contextualization of the gospel in the name of Anabaptism.

Were we (I was one of these missionaries) merely another of the crusading, church-planting "evangelical" missions preaching an individualistic, born again, personal experience with Christ apart from which individuals were heading for hell? To distinguish ourselves from this truncated view and establish our evangelical identity in the original sixteenth-century meaning of that word, we began to use the more inclusive term *Anabaptist*. In a word, we began to take "critical contextualization" of the gospel seriously. For those who were dissatisfied with the fundamentalistic "gospel" of individual salvation, the "Anabaptist Vision" as outlined by Harold Bender provided the perspective for an approach on the mission fields throughout the second half of the twentieth century.

The first Mennonite missionaries to Hokkaido (Mennonite Board of Missions) in the early 1950s, who went directly from Goshen Biblical Seminary, introduced an egalitarian concept of Christian community, strict biblicism, and nonresistance as the distinctive Anabaptist principles. Well into the 1970s the Japanese congregational leaders in Hokkaido were self-supporting, holding jobs that allowed them to give time to the church, and on principle they refused to be "ordained." At the same time, several of the first generation leaders in the Osaka and Kyushu area with the General Conference Mennonite mission were pressing these same non-institutional features as the marks of Anabaptism. In the 1980s, one of the major leaders in the Brethren in Christ Mission also began pressing the question what it means for Japanese churches to be Anabaptist.[12]

In the context of this cultural ferment, in 1986 I wrote a paper on "The Relevance of Anabaptism to Twentieth-Century Japanese Christianity" (unpublished). In it I raised the question whether a sixteenth-century European movement born in Christendom could be applied meaningfully in the Japanese culture, where the state religion was Shintoism and the dominant popular religion was Buddhism. If so, what elements might authentically represent the gospel? Similar questions were being raised in other Asian countries such as Indonesia and Australia.

Then in May 1986, the Asian Mennonite Conference was held in Taipei, Taiwan, which demonstrated the new mood that had come into existence among the Asian church bodies and marked the beginning of Asian leadership. This raised in a new way the question of common identity. The Asians' commonality was not marked by a shared "Asian" identity. Indeed, the primary language the delegates had in common was English! The representatives came from vastly different cultural settings. "Mennonites" around the world were a multilingual, multicultural multitude of varied socioeconomic status, moral values, social practices, interpretations of the Scripture, worship patterns, and understanding of discipleship.

It was at this conference that leadership shifted from mission boards' responsibility and financing to Asian church responsibility, from missionaries to the younger leaders of the Asian Mennonite churches. In a report to the Mennonite Board of Missions secretary for Asia I wrote, "The atmosphere of the conference was quite different from the one in Osaka in 1980. The old guard [dominated by missionary structures, financing, and goals] is out! There seems to be a new air of cautious realism and responsibility as the leadership shifts to younger Asian leaders." This signaled a redoubling of the search for a common self-identity as Mennonite churches, and the banner word for this identity became "anabaptism." Just how these various cultural expressions of church related to sixteenth-century European Anabaptism was not at all clear, but there was a sense that a generic anabaptism and "discipleship" could provide a unifying slogan. And this has become a developing reality in the Mennonite World Conference movement in the decades since.

What is Generic Anabaptism?

In the meantime here in the United States and in Europe, the interpretation of anabaptistic Mennonitism as an evangelical pacifistic, nonhierarchial (lay), socially concerned church group with emphasis on a Jesus-centered view of the Bible began to gain a hearing especially in academic religious centers. Through the centuries Anabaptists had been considered *Schwaermer* (fanatics), and their interpretations of Scripture were dismissed as "sectarian." Now scholars from other church traditions and perspectives on biblical interpretation began to take Anabaptist contributions to the discussion seriously.[13] So what precisely is generic anabaptism?

Anabaptism with a lower case "a" is a twentieth-century phenomenon—an attempt to adapt and adopt the insights and values of sixteenth-century Anabaptism as a guide to the interpretation and use of Scripture in our twenty-first century American culture. When it is written with a capital "A," it refers to the historical movement of sixteenth-century Europe, which developed as part of the Protestant Reformation. While contemporary generic anabaptism attempts to preserve an authentic continuation of the sixteenth-century movement, it is not and cannot be a replica of pristine Anabaptism. Rather, it represents a post-denominational perspective that seeks to dialogue across denominational lines.

Much has changed over the past five centuries. We live in vastly different political cultures than did the sixteenth-century Anabaptists. Historical studies have changed our way of understanding and interpreting the Scriptures. The concept of "Orthodoxy" with which the sixteenth century began no longer furnishes the paradigm for ecclesiastical relations. Both Protestant and Roman Catholic institutions have recognized the legitimacy of theological pluralism and the right of voluntary religious commitment. Scientific research and technological developments have altered our very way of life. Subtly these changes altered the cultural, political, and religious climate so that the conservative patterns of Amish and Mennonite communities less and less resemble the dynamic innovative responses of the original Anabaptists. This has introduced an ambiguity into claims on the Anabaptist label.

Within worldwide Mennonitism, there are two contemporary versions of Anabaptism, each claiming to be authentic representations of sixteenth-century Anabaptism. This complicates the task of defining the terms. While they have much common ground, at the same time they differ with each other concerning the nature of the Bible and its interpretation. The conservative groups assume a pre-critical view of Scripture and method of interpretation. Some of these conservative groups take a fundamentalist, charismatic perspective and some take a more traditional American Mennonite ("Old Orders") perspective. However, the biblical divide that separates both of these more traditional (pre-critical) Mennonite positions from present-day generic anabaptism is their view of the Bible. The fault line between the two versions lies along the historical distinction between the critical and pre-critical assumptions and methodologies brought to the interpretation of the Bible.[14]

Of course not all who take an anabaptist perspective in biblical interpretation are Mennonites, but anabaptistic Mennonitism as a participant in inter-denominational dialogue is an evangelical pacifistic, non-hierarchial (lay), socially concerned church group (denomination) with an emphasis on a Jesus-centered view of the Bible. This ecumenically oriented anabaptism is intellectually comfortable in the left wing of evangelical scholarship and does not draw sharp lines of distinction between its conservative and liberal interlocutors. It has a conservative but critical perspective on biblical interpretation, attempting to preserve and promote an authentic contemporary contextualization of the pre-critical hermeneutic of the sixteenth-century Anabaptists. It assumes that the Bible is the historical witness to and record of God's revelation through Israel that climaxed in Jesus who came as the Christ, the Son of God.

Various stages of this transition from a pre-critical to a critical approach to Scripture exist simultaneously among groups of contemporary Mennonites who themselves are at different stages of sociological accommodation to American culture. Historical groups of Hutterites, Amish, and "Old Order" Mennonites still claim to represent the true Anabaptist perspective. Other conservative Mennonite groups like the Evangelical Anabaptist Network, the Fellowship of [biblically] Concerned Mennonites, and other independent groups who have withdrawn from the main body over issues of biblical interpretation continue to regard the Bible as the infallible and literal Word of God. What these contemporary groups have in common is a hermeneutic that continues to view the meaning of Scripture through the lens of Protestant orthodoxy.

By way of comparison, the goal of generic anabaptism is not a fixed, uniform position. Its goal is not *orthodoxy* but *authenticity*—authentic interpretation of the Scripture through the lens of its own Anabaptist tradition. This necessitates a dialogue in two directions. First, a dialogue between sixteenth-century Anabaptism and twentieth-century Mennonitism, and second, a dialogue between twentieth-century Mennonitism and the other denominational traditions. At least implicitly, anabaptism recognizes that an authentic expression of Christ-centered faith as portrayed in the New Testament requires an inclusive conversational dialogue among all those seriously seeking to follow the way of Christ.

Generic anabaptism's dialogical character has resulted from the denominational rather than sectarian stance Mennonite bodies have adopted in the twentieth century and from their missionary activity crossing many different cultures. It became increasingly clear almost from the first that Western Mennonite interpretations and applications of the Bible did not always fit the diversity of cultural practices where they were planting churches. Neither could they give an effective interdenominational witness by pontificating a position. Effective witness needed to take a conversational, dialogical approach.

A Generic Anabaptist Hermeneutical Perspective

What then is the perspective that this generic anabaptism brings to the interpretation of the Bible? Again we must begin by noting that this is not an exclusively Mennonite perspective. Biblical students of one tradition and another share many of its understandings, but Anabaptism brings its own historical tradition to the dialogue.

Anabaptism does not establish a new orthodox creed for the universal church to follow. It does not establish a standardized theological and ethical formula to achieve uniformity among the diversity of the world's cultures. Rather, it is a perspective, a way of reading Scripture. It offers a way of reading and contextualizing Scripture under the tutelage of the Holy Spirit that adapts to multicultural dialogue. It makes Jesus the lens through which all Scripture is read, concentrating on the pattern of Jesus' life as the authentic example of God's will for human society. It offers a way to deal with the multicultural expressions of Christian faith in Jesus.

To further elucidate, perhaps we should begin with the conviction that *the Bible is the book of the church.*[15] This is a perspective that the Anabaptists inherited from and share with the Catholic tradition. The Bible is the inspired witness to and record of God's self-revelation to be interpreted and used as authority in the church. The books of Scripture issued out of the life and experience of Israel and the church, and the church created the Christian cannon, i.e., the list of recognized authoritative books. To speak with theological precision, the church does not give the canon its authority but recognizes its divine authority for the life of the church.

The warrant for this authority is found not so much in the text of the Bible as in the Spirit of God that initially inspired the text and is given to the church to guide it in understanding and use of the text. Today we refer to this as "contextualization" of the text—the interpretation and application of the text in different and changing cultural contexts. What does the Spirit intend in the original cultural context? What in the text transcends cultural differences, and what needs to be adapted to authentically preserve its original intention?

Both the Catholic and Anabaptist traditions recognize that this responsibility has been given to the church as the body of Christ, which continues the salvific work of the historical Jesus Christ. The Bible has not been given to individuals as a private revelation to provide a serendipitous authority and guidance. But here the Anabaptist and Catholic traditions have different perspectives. For Anabaptists the church is made up of voluntarily committed members who are full participants in the life of the church. This includes participation in discerning the spiritual meaning, relevance, and practical application of the text to specific situations.

To say that interpretation, which includes contextual theology and application, is basically the responsibility of Christian congregations living in the cultural situation does not mean that the congregation is a law unto itself! The congregation is dependent upon the ecclesial and scholarly resources at it disposal. The process of hermeneutical contextualization begins with the study of original languages, historical and anthropological studies of the biblical cultures, biblical translation, and theological evaluations, all of which require technical scholarly effort and insight. But at the end of the process it is the local congregation of Christian believers in the Spirit of Christ that is responsible to act in the name of Christ. This is a fundamental aspect of the historical Anabaptist perspective that generic anabaptism attempts to re-establish.

A second distinguishing perspective, one that marked the Anabaptists off from other Protestants, was their insistence that *because the New*

Testament is the record of God's revelation in Jesus, the Christ, it has authority over what preceded it. This was not merely a legalistic shift from the text of the Old to the text of the New. Rather, their new authority was Jesus, the Messiah, and not Moses, the Lawgiver.[16] Christians' mandate is to follow Jesus, and because the New Testament Scriptures are the trustworthy written witness to him, they are of supreme importance. They valued the Old as a preparatory document, the historical witness and record of God's covenant with Israel preparing the way for Christ and a new covenant to be written on the hearts of God's people, in the words of Jeremiah 31. The New Testament, they held, is the culmination of, fulfills, and serves as the interpretative key to the Old .

Protestant leaders, as Stuart Murray has pointed out,[17] continued the medieval pattern of appealing to the Old Testament law to establish a sociopolitical structure within which the church functioned. In effect they continued the social pattern in which the church (spiritual) and the state (secular) joined to establish a sacral community in which the civil structures for the total community were found in the Old Testament. The hermeneutical debate between Lutherans and Reformed merely continued the medieval argument whether the spiritual trumped the secular in authority, or vice versa, but both fully agreed that the Testaments—Old and New—shared an equal authority in the institutional church. Thus, for example, in Calvin's Geneva the church could render a judgment of heresy with the intention and full expectation of the death penalty to be carried out by the "Christian" government.

Anabaptists understood the New Testament to be a new covenant between God and humans creating a new people of God—a new social order. It was not merely a spiritual directive for individuals in their religious life, but a social directive to guide the ethical life of the human community. The Hebrew covenant is explicitly a religio-cultural covenant providing a sociopolitical structure for a people of God among the pagan nations of the earth. The New Testament gives little or no political instructions. Christians are simply to be "salt and light" for the world—a rather non-specific ethical directive. They are to follow the Spirit of agape according to the new ethical alternative taught for followers of "the Way." This raises the question of how the new Christian covenant is to be interpreted.

Protestant reformers held that the new covenant assumes and accepts the political context of the old, and merely provides for a midcourse correction and personalization of the relationship. Anabaptism, on the other hand, asserted that the new covenant establishes a new spiritual and cultural pattern based on the example of Jesus as "the true and living Way" (John 14:6). The church as the people of God under this new covenant is to be a voluntary alternative society taking its precedent from the New Testament. Where the New differs from the Old, Jesus' words, "It has been said by them of old . . . but I say unto you" are the authority for action. Christians are to be guided by a new ethical pattern. *Nachfolge Christi* (imitation of Christ) was not equated with patriotism in a Christian nation governed in the spirit and form of the Hebrew Scriptures.

The consequences of this hermeneutical revision of the Hebrew covenant had inevitable sociological implications. The government, which Paul says, "does not bear the sword in vain," was de-sacralized and understood as part of the fallen natural order. The secularization of the political order placed it outside the church, and in effect gave it the status of the pagan nations surrounding Israel. For the Anabaptists this created a tension between the true church and Christendom.

Although the first generation of Anabaptism did not function as a sectarian movement, it is well known that it became so in the centuries following. This is generally attributed to the social and political pressures that forced them to separate their societies from the continuing Christendom patterns of church and state. What has not been so clearly noted is that the old covenant is explicitly a sociocultural covenant creating a settled, national "people of God" among the pagan nations. The new covenant, on the other hand, assumes the dispersion of Israel as its metaphorical pattern. I mention this ambiguity in the Anabaptist interpretation of the relevance of the Old Testament because it has left contemporary generic anabaptism with a similar dilemma.

The Mennonite perspective on New Testament ethical interpretation led eighteenth- and nineteenth-century Mennonites to withdraw from the political society, which they called "the world." Where the example and teaching of Christ—understood as including the ethical admonition of the apostles—did not provide a practical political guide for action there was nothing to do but withdraw. Now that the Mennonite world has assimilated much of the professional, institutional, political, and economic ("world") culture, the relevance and role of the Old Testament is being reexamined. Generic anabaptism, however, maintains that Jesus as "pioneer and perfecter of the faith" is the ethical and spiritual gestalt and exemplar for Christian action.

That leads us to the third hermeneutical perspective of contemporary anabaptist biblical interpretation, namely, that *Jesus as the climax of revelation—the Word made flesh (John), and "image of the invisible God" (Paul)—is both the personal-spiritual and social-ethical pattern for Christians.* Evangelical Protestantism has interpreted Jesus as a spiritual redeemer and ideal for personal life but not an example to be followed in social ethics. Beginning with the original Protestant, Martin Luther, Jesus was understood to have had the unique "vocation" of Savior, a vocation, or calling, that his followers do not and cannot share. Although the spirit of Christ motivates lay Christians, the law of justice guides their secular functions in the world.

One can find beautiful passages in Luther's works extolling the nonresistant love of Jesus as an example for Christians to follow in their personal attitude, but alongside such passages are the exhortations to these same Christians to apply for the public job of hangman because as individuals of faith and love they bring the right spirit to the ghastly job. Jesus' call to "take up your cross and follow [my example]" does not apply to the Christian calling in the public arena. Discipleship is a matter of private faith and love.[18]

This perspective on Jesus' divine person and work on our behalf led Protestants to a focus on justification by faith-belief not by works-righteousness. Christ's role as God's penal substitutionary sacrifice became the almost exclusive center of interest, and our relation to him was interpreted as one of dependence and trust or *fiducia*—a favorite word of Luther. He remained focused on the cross and blood of Christ, made effective for lay Christians in the sacrament, rather than the ministry and lifestyle of Jesus that resulted in his execution as a religious and political threat. From this perspective the resurrection of Christ became the vindication of his divine self-sacrificial atoning death, not of his incarnational identification with us as the "true and living Way."[19]

The recognition of Jesus' sacrificial identification with us as God's "pioneer" (Heb. 12:2), and "servant" in whose likeness we are to be formed (Philippians 2: 6-8) is virtually ignored. His role as peacemaker is interpreted as a theological adjustment to satisfy the justice of God, and the ethical and social dimensions of peace making are muted. Salvation as reconciliation and transformation of human life and society through faithful commitment and enablement to follow his pattern—what one might call the "hermeneutics of reconciliation" is dismissed as "works righteousness." The classic tradition of *imitatio Christi* ("imitation of Christ") is rejected as a theological error of atonement theory and suspected as "works righteousness."

By contrast the Anabaptist tradition has from the beginning insisted that salvation is by faith alone, but "faith without works is dead." Faith is understood as faithfulness in following the Way marked out by Christ. It is not simply belief and trust in the merits of his substitutionary example. Following Christ who is the culmination of God's revelation is the essential core of Christian faith.

Finally, related closely to the above understanding of Jesus' pioneer role *is the concept of discipleship as* Nachfolge Christi—*the imitation of Christ.* Anabaptists understood discipleship as apprenticeship. A *disciple* is one who learns by following the example of the master, not merely by calling him lord, but by imitating his life style. A. M. Hunter caught the import of this anabaptist perspective when he entitled his exposition of the Sermon on the Mount *A Pattern for Life* (Westminster Press, 1953). Jesus is the "pioneer and perfecter of our faith" who set the pattern to be followed (Heb. 12:3ff). His endurance of society's hostility and, in the end, execution as a political criminal is understood as a personal-social path to be followed as a kind of discipline. To keep the faith means to persevere in this pattern modeled by Jesus.

The goal of biblical study, therefore, is not theoretical knowledge but practical behavior, namely, "justice, peace and joy in the Holy Spirit" (the spirit of Christ), as Paul wrote in Romans 14:17. Generic anabaptist hermeneutics is the "hermeneutics of obedience."[20] Its theology is a theology of apprenticeship. To be a Christian disciple means to participate in and live under the mandate of Jesus Christ, the Master, who not only leads but also enables and transforms us in and through the discipline of following.

In their literature, Anabaptists referred to this alternative way of living in society as taking up the cross and following Christ. They characterized the Christian life as the way of the cross, which is exemplified in the nonviolent lifestyle of Jesus. In this same manner, the anabaptist perspective interprets this call as a summons to the nonviolent lifestyle, or pattern of life, that led Jesus to the cross. It does not treat "cross bearing" (nonviolence) and "crucifixion of self" (self-denial) in the typical Protestant evangelical manner of simply equating it with self-denial. Certainly the nonviolent lifestyle of a peacemaker will often require self-denial, but not every act of self-denial can be identified as "taking up the cross and following Christ![21]

According to Matthew 28:20, from the Anabaptist perspective, the apostolic commission is to make followers of all the nations (*ta ethne*). Discipleship is not just for those of the Jewish nation but for all humankind! The Gentile nations are to be "apprenticed"—formed according to the archetypical pattern through following Jesus' lifestyle. They are to be inducted into the holy nation being formed under the new covenant (baptism), and instructed in the commandments and example of the Jesus ("teaching them"). This discipleship is not just the vocation of a special class—religious orders, pastors, and preachers. It is the pattern of the transformed life to which Christ calls everyone.

Such an anabaptist hermeneutical perspective calls for authentic contextualization of the message and example of Jesus in the tradition of the apostle Paul and first-century writers of Scripture. Indeed, the epistles of the New Testament themselves provide a model of such discernment and translation of the meaning of the life of Christ for the diverse cultures of the world. Given the inevitable diversity of world cultures in which the Christian Mennonite witness has taken root, the call to authentic discipleship as a hermeneutical principle becomes fundamental. We must again emphasize the guiding motto of Menno Simons: "Other foundation can no man lay than that is laid, which is Jesus Christ" (1 Cor. 3:11), and move forward under the aegis of the Holy Spirit of Christ.

"Bearing the heavy cross of Christ" was a favorite phrase of Menno to describe the martyr vocation of Christians. For him it clearly meant following the nonviolent pattern of Christ's life and patiently bearing the consequences. That he considered this the calling of every Christian with no exceptions is illustrated by his approach to the question whether a Christian could hold office as a magistrate, which he admitted is a "dangerous office." He did not give a direct answer with scriptural proofs. He simply insisted that whether a person is ordained of God to be king, magistrate, or judge, as a Christian he is first called to follow the word and example of Christ in that office. There are no exceptions. Indeed, we might well end this essay by quoting from his *Reply to False Accusations* [that Anabaptists will not obey the magistrate].

> Henceforth, beloved rulers, see to it, you who call yourselves Christian, that you may be that also in deed and in word. Water, bread, wine, and the name do not make a Christian, but those are Christian who are born of God, are of a divine spirit and nature, are of the same mind as Christ Jesus . . . love their neighbors as themselves; lead an unblamable, regenerate, pious life, and willingly walk in the footsteps of Christ. . . . These the Word of God calls Christians.[22]

Notes

1. In her unpublished dissertation, "The Articulation of Mennonite Beliefs about Sexuality 1890-1930" (May 2003), 93, Brenda Martin Hurst traces the explicit teaching of the covering as a biblical ordinance to John S. Coffman. She writes, "The cap became a 'prayer head covering' symbolizing a woman's submission to God's order of authority: God, Christ, Man, Woman."

2. Mumaw, John, *Preach the Word: Expository Preaching from the Book of Ephesians* (Herald Press: Scottdale, Pa, 1987) attempted both by homiletical instruction and example to advocate expository preaching in Mennonite pulpits.

3. Daniel Kauffman, *Mennonite History, Including a Brief Sketch of the Church from the Time of Christ* (Scottdale, Pa.: Mennonite Publishing House, 1927), 48.

4. Ibid. p. 49.

5. C. Henry Smith, *The Story of the Mennonites,* 3rd. ed. (Newton, Kan.: Mennonite Publication Office, 1950), 4.

6. See "Character of the Evangelical Anabaptists," 293-298. (Scottdake, Pa.: 1942).

7. *Conrad Grebel c. 1498-1526: The Founder of the Swiss Brethren Sometimes Called Anabaptists* (Goshen, Ind.: The Mennonite Historical Society, 1950), 209-10.

8. The proper interpretation of nonresistance and its biblical basis became a focal issue in this debate. Guy F. Hershberger's argument that both testaments teach nonresistance was strongly refuted by John L. Stauffer, president of Eastern Mennonite School, and an ardent premillennialist. See his "The Error of Old Testament Nonresistance," in *The Sword and Trumpet* 28.2 (1960): 6-16, later published posthumously in 1971 as a pamphlet entitled *The Message of Scripture on Nonresistance*. John R. Mumaw published a pamphlet, *Nonresistance and Pacifism* (Mennonite Publishing House: Scottdale, Pa. 1952) arguing against a more vague presentiment that an activist "anabaptist" nonviolence was leading to liberal pacifism. And the *Sword and Trumpet* kept up a steady barrage of articles presenting a traditional literalistic Mennonite interpretation, implicitly if not always explicitly critical of the emphasis on Anabaptism.

9. See my "American Mennonites and the Bible, 1750-1950," first published in the *Mennonite Quarterly Review,* 1967, and reprinted in *Essays on Biblical Interpretation Anabaptist-Mennonite Perspectives,* ed. Willard M. Swartley (Elkhart, Ind.: Institute of

Mennonite Studies, 1984), 131-150 for more detail on this period.

10. That this is indeed the intention of the *Confession's* authors is illustrated by other significant changes. For example, in contrast to the Garden City confession (1921), which declared the seven day creation account to be "an historic fact and literally true," it speaks of God as the infinite Creator, source and end of all things, and of creatures as limited and dependent upon God. It speaks of revelation as "supremely and finally [given] in His incarnate Son," and it bases Scripture's authority on its witness to Christ, who is the "key to [its] proper understanding". The command to nonresistance is based on Christ's redeeming love and sovereignty overall men [sic]", and nonconformity to the world is described in terms of spiritual allegiance to Christ's kingdom, not hortatory texts from Scripture.

11. *Confession of Faith in a Mennonite Perspective*, published by arrangement with the General Board of the General Conference Mennonite Church and the Mennonite Church General Board (Scottdale, Pa: Herald Press, 1995), 8.

12. At the time the Brethren In Christ missionaries had chosen not to emphasize the connection of Japanese congregations with an American denomination. This led some of the Japanese leaders to search for their identity among the many Christian groups. Unsatisfied with the Fundamentalism of the Japan Evangelical Association, and aware of their Mennonite relations, they were exploring the Anabaptist alternative that was being tendered.

13. People like Stanley Hauerwas, who calls himself a "camp follower," and Richard Hays at Duke University, Christopher Rowland and Stuart Murray of England, James McClendon Jr., Glen Stassen, Nancy Murphy, and the like from Evangelical backgrounds began to accept anabaptism as a dialogical partner. See the October 2000 issue of *The Mennonite Quarterly Review* 54.4.

14. . In his chapter, "Evangelical Reconstruction of the Anabaptist Vision," Levi Miller writes, "A reconstructed understanding of evangelical Anabaptism would be completely at home within the basic theological categories of Protestant orthodoxy. . . . An evangelical Anabaptism for the next century will embrace an orthodox Christianity, holy living and intimacy with God, along with an ethic of nonresistance, peace and justice"; *Refocusing A Vision: Shaping Anabaptist Character in the 21st Century*, ed. John. D. Roth (Goshen, Ind.: Mennonite Historical Society, 1995), 31, 34. Miller takes his stand with the "pre-critical" hermeneutic of orthodox Protestantism and interprets any revision of it as a watering down of "transcendent and revealed biblical Christianity." Scholars, he continues, who deny or reject such "revealed biblical Christianity" can still be accepted as anabaptist "if the author—especially if the author has Mennonite parents—still believes in pacifism, ecological wholeness, or perhaps liberation and justice." 29. These comments illustrate well the character of the divergence that separates the two versions of generic anabaptism.

15. In Article 4 on Scripture, the 1995 *Confession* states that the Bible is "the essential book of the church" after affirming its inspiration and trustworthiness as the "Word of God written." An earlier edition sent to the constituencies for testing made the statement the lead sentence for the article, but in both editions the point is clear. The Bible is an instrument of the Holy Spirit to nurture "the obedience of faith to Jesus Christ and guide the church in shaping its teaching, witnessing, and worship," 22.

16. Menno Simons has a particularly clear reference to this in his discussion of the

swearing of oaths: "The Scripture teaches that we should hear Christ . . . . [and] Christ Jesus does not in the New Testament point His disciples to the Law in regard to the matter of swearing . . . but He points us now from the Law to yea and nay, as to the dispensation of perfectness [sic]. . . ."; *The Complete Writings of Menno Simons, c. 1496-1561*, ed. John C. Wenger (Scottdale, Pa.: Herald Press, 1956), 518.

17. Stuart Murray, *Biblical Interpretation in the Anabaptist Tradition* (Pandora Press: Kitchener, Ont., 2000), 223. See also his chapter on "The Two Testaments."

18. Carl F. H. Henry's two volumes on Christian Ethics are a contemporary example of this kind of emphasis. In 1957 he published his 690-page *Christian Personal Ethics* with the promise that a volume on social ethics would follow. Finally, seven years later in 1974 he published a 190-page volume entitled *Aspects of Christian Social Ethics* (both published by Eerdmans).

19. One might refer to this as the "hermeneutics of justification." The concept of "justification by faith alone" (*sola fide*) dominated Protestant interpretation of passages where "righteousness/justice, peace and reconciliation were the subject.

20. Murray, *Biblical Interpretation*, 225.

21. For example, in a recent seminar in Northern Ireland my appeal to "the way of the cross" as the call to nonviolence prompted an objection from one of the participants. He pointed out that his friend had felt called to volunteer for military duty in the Iraqi war as a matter of cross-bearing. He considered his willingness to deny himself personal security in order to help violently overthrow Saddam's regime an example of bearing his cross. While respecting the sincerity of his sacrifice, one cannot but remember Jesus' word to Peter when he reached for his sword in the Garden. The defense of Jesus with the sword at the risk of his own life did not qualify as "taking up his cross" as 1 Peter 2:21-25 so eloquently states.

22. *Complete Writings*, 553.

3

The Role of Mennonite Theological Inquiry in the Coming Decades

The Contemporary Situation

Recently when looking through old files in connection with an essay I was writing, I found a scrap of paper on which I had written a quote from H. S. Bender. He said, "Theology is like washing dishes. It is necessary, but we should not confuse it with the feast!" That is very true, but when the sink and all the workspace in the kitchen is so full of dirty dishes that you do not have space to get the next meal, it is time to wash the dishes. We need some clean dishes.

In the twenty-first century we face a new, dynamic, cross-cultural worldwide Mennonite church at a time when North Americans still have not seriously worked at the theological divergence among ourselves. We have tried to gather under a common Anabaptist heritage with slogans and ambiguous biblical terminology but have not dealt with the issues raised by our secular culture or the pluralism of global culture. We have assumed an implicit traditional theology and approached immediate practical ethical and social problems within the framework of that theology. We find ourselves without an adequate "anabaptist"[1] hermeneutical and theological methodology to accommodate this pluralism.

To a considerable extent the clash of theological positions in North America itself is a clash of traditional rational theology that seeks its values in the past with an empirical perspective that looks forward to an open future. Not only is the mixture of the traditional and the empirical in our own theology often self-contradictory and confused, now it must attempt to interface with cultural faiths of fundamentally different presuppositions. The attempt to meld the traditional values and theologies of African, Asian, and South American Mennonites with those of North America has only exacerbated this theological situation.

As introduced and elaborated in chapter 2 of this volume, we have inherited a theological situation that grew out of the coalescence of traditional Mennonitism and American Fundamentalism at the beginning of the twentieth century. Mennonite leaders took their cues from the Fundamentalists and thought of theology as simply a re-statement of "Bible doctrine"—a title often used in their publications. According to Fundamentalism, theology's task is the organization and presentation of biblical doctrines, and its ultimate purpose is the orthodox statement of beliefs, or dogma, necessary for salvation. Unaware how much their presuppositions and methodology were a product of Western rationalism, these fundamentalist leaders rather naively claimed the Bible as their only theological textbook. They read it as divinely inspired texts that could be used to prove true doctrine. Indeed, at its populist base the Bible teachers were claiming that the King James Version was inspired scriptural text.[2]

At mid-twentieth century the Mennonite perspective was in danger of eroding in the face of Fundamentalism's ascendancy in America. As the early twentieth-century American Mennonites were becoming assimilated into American Protestantism, they were in grave danger of being cut off from their own historical tradition, which admittedly had wandered into the eddies of history. They were tempted to substitute a modern fundamentalist definition of the faith for their hermeneutical perspective on Scripture. This Fundamentalism virtually ignored the great theological tradition of the church and appealed to a truncated version of orthodox Reformed (Calvinistic) theology and a pietistic/revivalist version of the faith experience.[3] Harold S. Bender's "Anabaptist Vision" was an attempt to rekindle the authentic biblical perspective of our tradition, and it was by no means uncontested in the decades immediately following its publication.

In the past seventy-five years, Mennonite scholars have majored in historical studies of both the Reformation and the Bible, and it is no secret that they have been suspicious of theology as such.[4] Actually, however, they have done a great deal of surreptitious theology in their historical studies. From John Horst, who interpreted the Anabaptists as sixteenth-century fundamentalists, through Bender who emphasized their biblicism and free church character, to Friedman who characterized their theology as "existential" or experience centered, to Wenger, Yoder, Klaassen, and Augsburger, we have been introduced to a variety of implicit theologies! Indeed, it took a non-church historian like James Stayer with his polygenesis interpretation of Anabaptism to awaken us to the theological bias of our introspective approaches to history.

This contemporary Mennonite appeal to Anabaptist history, which began already at the turn of the twentieth-century with the generation of John S. Coffman and Menno Steiner, has been of incalculable value in shaping the twentieth century vision of Mennonites. It has helped us to more critically evaluate the character of the American culture in which we live. It has led us to a new and enhanced understanding of Scripture. I would in no way denigrate this important development. My contention is that simply clarifying and understanding the past, whether it is the Reformation or the Bible, does not give us a self-evident theological positioning of the gospel in contemporary secular society.

Getting in touch with the past is crucial to its authentic continuation, but "biblical studies" and "historical investigation" are not enough. We cannot maintain authentic continuity by merely using the biblical or orthodox terminology. We cannot adequately meet the challenges of contemporary society by simply repeating "biblical language," or insisting on duplicating its worldview and dealing with issues raised in past historical situations. When we try to do this, biblical meanings become distorted, and theological rationalizations become anachronistic. We become irrelevant to the contemporary situation. We need to do for the twenty-first century what Anabaptists did for the sixteenth. We must make constructive, critical theological discernment and cultural adaptation. A contemporary constructive theological quest based on the Bible and informed by church tradition is fundamental to the search for an authentic expression of the kingdom message of Jesus.

Why Emphasize Constructive Theology?

The primary concern to reposition the Bible, i.e., to read it in the context and from the perspective of the contemporary cultural situation, does not grow out of a rationalistic or "liberal" view that contemporary secular values should be determinative. Neither is it to harmonize the biblical message with the concepts of other religious cultures. Rather, it is a concern for self-understanding and authentic re-presentation of the scriptural message.

The need for contextualization stems from the historical nature of revelation itself and from a concern for the witness of the church to the many cultures of our world. God is and can be known only from within historical cultural reality, and that cultural reality must be one's own, not that of someone else. God's self-communication, i.e., the *Theos* in theology, is unalterably tied to our personal experience of reality. Knowledge of God's reality cannot be imposed as a universal rational generalization or logical conclusion. It comes as an existential gift, as a response to "witness," or "calling" in a cultural mode ("language") we can understand. Hence, the continuing need for a contextual repositioning of the original disclosure remains necessary.

Christians claim that God's ultimate disclosure has come to us in a historical embodiment ("incarnation") within ancient Hebrew-Jewish culture that is witnessed to in the biblical record. The original logos (Word) was not essentially a rational verbal statement to be proclaimed and taught in philosophical schools, but an embodiment in the historical situation of near eastern society. Coming as it has in a specific time and place, not as a universal idea but a historical embodiment, the disclosure has the inevitable marks of a local phenomenon that can only be perpetuated in the form of witness, not theoretical argument. This witness tells what has happened in the past that continues to condition the evolving cultural experience. It is not, however, merely an appeal to past reality, but a demonstration of that reality in the evolving present. The place and role of theology, therefore, should be located within this circle of witness. It is not primarily an academic intellectual exercise, but an integral aspect of the witness.

A constructive contextualization must engage theological and ethical questions such as the following in our Western world. To what extent are we limited to the first- and second-century concepts and ontological assumptions in describing the nature of God and the relation of Deity to humanity? To what extent are we limited to the time, place, and process of the Genesis creation stories in our understanding of the origins of the universe and human beings? How is our understanding of "peace" and reconciliation to God tied to a monarchical social order and the biblical imagery of blood sacrifice? How much should the taboos of ancient Hebrew culture control our concepts of sexuality and the relationship of men and women in society?

Reckoning with such questions is fundamental to a constructive theological process, and we have been very reluctant to face them directly. Our churches have appealed to literal statements from the biblical text or preferred to make general "biblical" statements, which in themselves are often open to more than one interpretation, and let individuals wrestle with the theological and ethical implications for themselves. When we do not deal with such elemental questions of hermeneutical and theological methodology, the church is at a great disadvantage in dealing with questions raised by scientific research and by social and moral issues.

Once we have decided to tackle these issues, there is still the question raised by the present cultural pluralism, namely, how much uniformity can or should we expect as Mennonite theologies develop in this current century? If, as I have suggested, doing theology is a process of repositioning the gospel in the variety of world cultures, it would seem to follow that we cannot expect to arrive at one universal systematic Mennonite orthodoxy for our international, cross-cultural denomination. A twenty-first century Schleitheim declaration of beliefs would have to encompass a much wider scope of diversity than the sixteenth-century one did!

In any case I am persuaded that a universal dogma is not the ultimate goal of the theological process. Rather, the purpose is authentic contextual embodiment of the new reality, which was supremely embodied in Jesus. The situations in North America, Asia, and Africa, for example, require quite different approaches—what Kosuke Koyama once called the difference between "hamburger theology" and "sushi theology." One would expect considerably more uniformity within any given culture than across cultures.

What we should expect and work for across cultural boundaries is a mutual sharing and fructifying of our provincial theologies. And Western orthodoxy is provincial! Thus far the sharing process has generally traveled in one direction from West to East and South. It must go both ways! Asia, Africa, Latin America have much to teach us about the work of God and the terminology to express it in theological witness. For example, the Ethiopian mother's use of a "story" to answer a child's question can be very helpful in understanding the role of the creation stories. Unfortunately, under the guise of conservative Western theology, American evangelicals have exported a rationalistic, pseudo-empirical interpretation of the biblical stories that may sound the same on the surface but is far different in its ramifications.

A related question has to do with the theological essence and content that can give authentic identity to the world Mennonite conglomerate in the coming decades. Does our historical experience suggest a content focus? A methodology? A hermeneutical orientation? Are there special insights, questions, and issues that might identify us? Is there what we might call a theological bias that legitimately characterizes the identity and role of the church? Is peace and reconciliation our ethical hallmark? If the latter is so, I might add, we must do an even more comprehensive theological critique and construction than we have done thus far.

Theology and the Bible

In the perspective of Anabaptist-Mennonite theology, two further substantive considerations urgently present themselves. These have to do with the constituent nature of the theological process. Both of them stem from the essentially historical nature of God's self-disclosure. The first has to do with the relation of contemporary theology to the Bible as a historical record. The second has to do with the role of theology as part of the church's ongoing witness.

Anabaptist-Mennonite church life has been tied in a distinctive way to the Bible. Conservative theologians in the tradition of Protestant Orthodoxy also place emphasis on the Bible, but it has functioned for them as a theological source book. Biblical theology has been the forte of the Reformed biblical scholars. Anabaptist-Mennonite tradition has viewed the Bible much more as a general guidebook for life and morals. While they would not have explained it that way, Mennonites tended to read the Bible more as a historical than a theological document. For them the Bible presented a view of human life in history which was to be emulated, and the church's connection to that historical reality was not primarily an intellectual-theological worldview to be believed but an experiential continuation of the living reality in history. Their criterion, therefore, has been authenticity and not orthodoxy. Theology in such a tradition stands in the interface between the original witness and the contemporary church's life and witness. Its role is to express an authentic cultural translation of the original in the spirit of Jesus.

Scripture is a historical record, the book of the church, not a supernatural oracle of theological texts. Only secondarily the revelatory logos resulted in the gathering of a Scripture which attempts to explain and guide the church's existence and witness. The original Christian movement was the womb of Scripture's inception. The New Testament writings are a kind of theological expression of that original community's faith and the instrument of its witness. They are not primarily private religious devotional texts to inspire reverence and worship, or theoretical religious and ethical discourses to stimulate intellectual discussion. They are models of the newly formed theological community at work giving witness to the historical event that formed it into a "new humanity." They reflect the faith and life of the new resurrection phenomenon, and become the touchstone for all continuing theological efforts. The theological task, therefore, is to facilitate the authentic continuity of this original vision and possibility for humanity.

When Scripture is read as a historical document, we must pay attention to its cultural characteristics. We must first read the text as an ancient record and witness. The more recent canonical criticism does not cancel the basic necessity of historical criticism. The Bible's message is presented in the thought patterns, presuppositions, and literary genre of ancient Near Eastern cultures. Historical narrative and myth are interwoven with parable, poetry, symbolism, oracle, allegory—all this in a sacral setting. Its ethical and spiritual admonitions presuppose the moral structures, the scientific presuppositions and socioeconomic relationships of the time. Its doctrinal instruction is cast in the framework of local issues, e.g., Jew and Gentile, "clean and unclean," and reflects pre-Copernican concepts of the cosmos.

Having been written in different times and places, its message as well as its literary style is multiform not uniform. It is not only multiform in its literary character—poetry, oracle, myth, historical event, legislation—it presents us with multicultural theological metaphors. For example, there is little or no attempt to bring the different concepts of God into a comprehensive coherent whole. God is merciful Father and vengeful Tyrant, sovereign Creator and frustrated Sustainer, strict Lawgiver and indulgent Parent, transcendent Mystery and intimate Friend. This multi-conceptualization of God has been a problem to the intellectual thinkers of the church since the first centuries. Indeed, Marcion in the second century contended that the God of the Old Testament could not be the same as the Father of Jesus Christ.

Upon reflection it should be obvious that this is the only way a truly historical disclosure of the divine mystery could be given, but we have been exceedingly slow to acknowledge the implications of this for its use today. What is being revealed must connect with and have meaning within a given human cultural context to be a genuine communication. As mentioned earlier, one theologian once pointed out that if the Genesis stories about the origins of the earth had been cast in twentieth-century scientific terms, they would have had virtually no meaning for those who lived before the twentieth century.

This historical character of revelation itself implies both the possibility and necessity of contextualization and constructive theology. The fact that the message of the Bible is itself expressed in several different cultural settings and languages clearly implies that the communication of God's Word is not confined or limited to the language and cosmology of any one time, place, or culture in the ancient past. In contrast to the Koran, for example, which can only be conveyed in the sacred language of its Arabic text, the Bible can be contextualized without diluting its message. Indeed, the New Testament is a Graeco-Roman contextualization of a preceding Hebrew-Jewish phenomenon, and we must continue to contextualize it if we are to obey the messianic commission.

Critical contextualization, therefore, necessitates not only the reconstruction of the ancient meaning of the text but the construction of its contemporary parallel. We are not limited to the ancient forms of expression among the pluralistic cultures of our contemporary world. As cultural presuppositions, definitions, patterns, and understandings change it is the role of theology in a believers church tradition to construct contemporary parallels authentic to the spirit and message of the Bible. The church uses Scripture to understand, guide, and further its life and work under the continuing aegis of the Spirit.

Theology as Church Process and Mission

As we have noted, the primary result of the historical embodiment of the Word was the formation of a human community, namely, the *ecclesia* of those willing to become disciples of Jesus. The authentic continuation of the original revelation is to be found in this historical-sacramental movement which we call the "body of Christ." In this regard the sixteenth-century Anabaptist movement was nearer to the Catholic position than to contemporary Protestant individualism, and the historical experience of the Roman Church has much to teach us on this point. If the Mennonite church is to be authentically Anabaptist, it must take itself seriously as a theological community. Constructive theological work is not simply or even primarily the task of the academic community. It is the work of the witnessing church. As Andrew Kirk puts it in his *The Mission of Theology and Theology as Mission* (1997), theology is very much a part of the mission of the church.

The historical character of God's salvation in Christ necessarily implies that we play a participatory role in the ongoing reconciliation initiated by Jesus in his life, death, and resurrection. In the words of Paul, we are to "fill up the sufferings of Christ" (Col. 1:24). We are not only recipients of salvation, but we become part of a movement for the reconciliation of humankind. Christ is the "pioneer" of our faith. He established the new paradigm. He has opened the way to God. He is the true and living way. We follow in his way of peace and peacemaking, and according to Jesus' own words we are to "do greater things" than he did.

Here let me make a brief more philosophical observation concerning Christology. The difference that Christ made is very real, but it is a difference in history, not in a mythical realm that we reify with the language of substance ontology. Theologies that work from Greek ontological presuppositions attempt to define the work of Christ with the terminology of substance ontology to maintain its "reality." This is understandable, but it has become especially problematic in our empirically oriented world, since "ontological" and "empirical," "reality" and "fact" are ambiguously confused! To illustrate, a noted evangelical scholar vigorously objected to my statement that Jesus' deity was not empirical in the same sense that his humanity was, and many of my less sophisticated critics simply assumed that "ontological" meant real. Thus when I critically analyzed the use of substance ontology as a christological category, they assumed that I was denying the reality of Jesus' divinity.

Rather, the distinction that we need to make is between the mythical as a heuristic category, which presupposes dualism, and the historical as an ontological sign. Our Christian tradition affirms the ontological reality of historical existence. In this it differs widely from religions like Hinduism in which history is *maya*, or illusion. In contrast to the Hindu avatar, which is a mythical incarnation, Christian theology affirms a relation of God to the world, which makes possible a real, ontological embodiment of God's active presence in history. Christ's work was not mythical in character, but truly historical, i.e., ontologically real in the spatio-temporal (secular) sense of the word. Neither was it primarily a mystical, spiritual negotiation within the life of Deity, but rather a personal-social embodiment such as defines historical existence.

The reason for this christological digression is to establish the significance of life in the church as the primary, sacramental witness to the reality of Christ, who is the embodiment of God's active presence in history. Such a reality remains real only in the ongoing personal-social processes of human history. The presence and ministry of Jesus, the Christ, is alive today in and through us by his Spirit. If there is no authentic continuity between his ministry of reconciliation and the *ecclesia* of those who are his followers—participants in the body of Christ—then he is not alive in any historical sense, and our theology will be vacuous and unconvincing.

The living human community, which receives and responds to the disclosure, is the primary instrument or medium of historical revelation. Thus the church as the living continuation of the historically experienced event is itself the bridge to the original revelation. The church is the demonstrative witness to the reality of the first-century Jesus, whom it confesses to be both God's Messiah and ruler of the world. It re-presents the original reality in the contemporary cultural settings. As such the church willy-nilly is the context within which the message of the Bible becomes credible or incredible. The Bible is the book of the church, its essential handbook and constitutive record.[5] As the interface between the original historical disclosure (Christ) and contemporary church life (body of Christ), the theological process is first one of understanding its "handbook and record," then of pointing to an authentic corresponding possibility in the present.

This ecclesia is not merely a mystical reality ("communion of saints") or theological concept, but a living, secular community of the

Spirit of Christ. Being a historical, cultural community, this body unavoidably changes with the evolutionary development of human society. It cannot be changeless. Only the Christ, "the Alpha and Omega," is changeless. The body cannot preserve its original purity by enunciating a changeless orthodox creed or by creating an infallible institutional form. Both have been tried and have failed. Change is inevitable and inescapable. But perhaps more germane for us, neither can it preserve its original character by maintaining a simple biblical primitivism. The Spirit of Christ is promised to the church to enable and guide it as it endeavors to be faithful to the original witness.

The theological process is the dialogue that goes on within the church as it seeks to discern the voice of the Spirit. It requires at least a modicum of agreement on hermeneutical method, ecclesiastical self-identity and assumptions, and the identification of questions and issues. In this sense the community of the Spirit precedes the theological process. A theological community is not created by the uniformity of its doctrines but reflects shared values and concerns of the community in theological process.

Theology, then, is crucial to the life and witness of the church. If the church is to be an authentic continuation of the sacramental embodiment of God in Christ, it must not merely mimic the ancient original. Rather it must be a living, contemporary expression of that same presence. The theological process of repositioning the message of the gospel in changing cultures is critical to an authentic contextualized expression of God's kingdom among us.

In the Anabaptist tradition, we have always had to live with pluralism both inside and outside the community. The original sixteenth-century movement itself was a diverse movement, not a tidy unified community. The nature and extent of diversity that can be accommodated is part of the theological dialogue. At what point does radical pluralism dissolve the community into a dysfunctional mass? Certainly we are not willing to settle for a radical reconstitution of community—a community of doubt rather than faith, of pragmatic humanistic values rather than "theonomous" values, a community of individuals sharing their private mystical experiences.[6] But can we see ourselves as a theological community gathered in dialogue around the Scriptures, unified in our attempt to frame and resolve the right questions rather than insisting on the right answers? It is my conviction that only a continued theological focus on *loyalty to Jesus of Nazareth as the messianic Son of God* will unify the worldwide Anabaptist-Mennonite movement in an authentic witness in the decades ahead.[7]

In summary, then, the basic role of the theological process is to first understand the original record and second to transmit it into the contemporary situation. Theology is first of all a word to and for the church, then also for the worldly cultures. It attempts to put into words and concepts the reality presented in the Bible so that the church may be an authentic continuation of the biblical reality. Then it also attempts to declare that same reality to the world as it is confessed and lived out in the church. Thus as a churchly function it verbally locates the message in the world. Contemporary Mennonite scholarship has worked hard at the first part of this task but has given far less attention to the latter task.

Notes

1. See my chapter in this volume entitled, "Interpreting the Bible: Anabaptist or Mennonite."

2. Mennonite teachers generally followed this literalistic lead although they continued to read Scripture in their traditional way on matters of nonconformity and nonresistance. Some leaders like Bishop George R. Brunk (I), who wrote a small book, *Rightly Dividing the Scriptures: Gospel Synergism* (Fentress, Va.: The Sword and Trumpet, 1935) to counter the booklet of the same title by C. I. Scofield, claimed that the problem with Fundamentalism was that it was not fundamental enough, and he said that Mennonites were teaching the "all things."

3. The Mennonite confession adopted in 1921 was called "Christian Fundamentals: Articles of Faith." For a more detailed survey of the shifting theological climate in the Mennonite Church see my chapter, "Shifting Mennonite Theological Orientations," in *Anabaptist-Mennonite Identities in Ferment,* Occasional Papers No. 14, ed. Leo Driedger and Leland Harder (Elkhart, Ind.: Institute of Mennonite Studies, 1990).

4. In the early 1950s, when the Goshen Biblical Seminary faculty was discussing the name for our new post-college training program, H. S. Bender, dean of the newly formed seminary, insisted that it should be "Biblical" and not "Theological" Seminary. He associated theology with rational intellectual disciplines that too often went beyond Scripture.

5. In an early version of the 1995 *Confession of Faith,* the committee introduced the article on Scripture with the words, "The Bible is the book of the church," but in the final edition made it the concluding paragraph explaining that this means that the church has the responsibility of interpreting it.

6. On the one hand, we are not willing, in the words of one Unitarian Universalist congregation, to simply be a group "nurturing one another's diverse spiritual paths in a warm, friendly, family atmosphere." On the other hand, neither are we ready to fol-

low the example of the Southern Baptist Convention's more recent fundamentalistic literalism, which demands compliance with first-century church conventions that represent an ancient expression of the gospel.

7. The "Seven Core Convictions" adopted for study at the Mennonite World Conference in 2003 seem to move in this direction. Crucial to their theological impact, however, will be their continued use as a basis for dialogue and discernment. It is interesting, for example, that conviction 4 highlights *the Bible* rather than the Holy Spirit. How do we understand the Holy Spirit's role in the contextualization of Scripture?

4

Pacifism and Nonviolence: Reassessing the Paradigms

A presentation to an interdisciplinary seminar, Union Theological College, Belfast, 2003

Since this is not a debate or an attempt to convert, but a fraternal discussion of a difficult and anguishing subject in which we are all existentially involved, I will not frame my comments as an apologetic for pacifism. Rather, I will begin with a brief confessional account of the Mennonite position and end with reflections on the nature of the argument for nonviolence as the vocation of the church.

There is great variety in pacifistic positions today, from Tolstoy's literalistic nonresistance to Gandhi's nonviolent resistance, from the "Refusenicks" of the Vietnam War ("Hell no! We won't go!") to the selective refusal of just war advocates. I come from an old and honorable tradition known as Anabaptism. Today the tradition is most immediately associated with Mennonites of various denominations and is often associated with quietism and social withdrawal—"*die Stille im Lande.*" In the Mennonite tradition we have not usually spoken of our position as pacifism but as "nonresistance," making Matthew 5:38 as traditionally translated our identifying text: "But I say to you, do not resist evil [or, an evildoer]. But if anyone strikes you on the right cheek, turn the other also." We have traditionally identified pacifism with liberalism and social gospel and have argued vigorously for a "biblical nonresistance."

The earliest Anabaptists accepted the two-kingdom dualism adapted by Luther and Calvin from the medieval classification of "temporal and spiritual" realms. They spoke of the two kingdoms as "church and world." The church was made up of those who voluntarily chose to be baptized, and this ecclesial community was identified with Christ's kingdom. According to the 1527 Schleitheim Confession, those who were not baptized into the church on the voluntary confession of faith were living in the world "outside the perfection of Christ." This was the sphere in which the state ruled by violent coercion. Those who chose baptism chose to become followers of Christ's nonresistant way of life.

When severe persecution, which lasted several centuries, excluded them from participation in society, they separated themselves physically from the "world" and tried to form peaceful communities that would not replicate the coercive, violent patterns of society "outside the perfection of Christ." (Anabaptists were forcibly removed to rural areas in the mountains of Switzerland, and the citizens of both the Reformed and Roman Catholic faiths avoided all possible contact with them.) Since they were ostracized, they made it their mission to be candles in the dark, or "cities set on a hill" letting their light shine so that others would glorify the Father in heaven. I'm sure I need not point out the danger of self-righteousness immanent in such a self-image of the church!

Needless to say, they did not fully succeed in establishing totally nonresistant religious communities. In Russia the German-speaking Mennonite Colonies of the nineteenth century had to form a self-regulating police force to keep order among Mennonite petty criminals; and when the Bolshevik revolution threatened the very existence of the colonies, some of them organized self-defense forces—with disastrous results. In less dramatic situations, the withdrawn communities depended on the sanction of gossip and exclusion (the ban) to regulate community behavior. When public laws were infringed, they relied on the worldly police force to deal with the matter. In Mennonite circles we often argued whether use of the police—such as when one caught a thief in the chicken house—was consistent with our nonresistance, and stories were told of farmers who had caught neighbors stealing and actually "heaped coals of fire on their heads."

Mennonites' withdrawal from responsibility for the larger sociopolitical community while at the same time depending on its police and defense forces gave our pacifism a passive and reactive character, and during times of crisis we were accused of cowardice and disloyalty. This passive and reactionary character may already seem to be implied in the negative statement of the doctrine as *non*resistance, although it was not so intended or applied. Someone has noted that calling the Christian's lifestyle "nonresistant" or "nonviolent" is about like describing marriage as "non-adultery." We constantly referred to it as a lifestyle and sought to live that way.

During World War I, Mennonites in the United States were forced into the military, and when they would not cooperate they were imprisoned. When the universal draft was enacted at the beginning of the World War II, church leaders, along with the Quakers and the Church of the Brethren, worked out an arrangement with the government whereby Mennonite young men and other conscientious objectors could serve in a Civilian Public Service Corp without government remuneration. The church largely financed this arrangement.

Following World War II, Mennonites have become known for their more proactive attempts at peace building. Through a major cooperative effort of some twenty different Mennonite denominations known as Mennonite Central Committee they have worked "*im Namen Christi*" (the MCC motto) literally around the world to identify with and serve those who suffer injustice and deprivation, which are root causes of conflict. The Mennonite social services mission in the world made Matthew 25:31-46 its golden text. In this Mennonites have tried to be proactive, tackling the problems inherent in systemic violence. We have moved beyond relief into nonviolent development and peace building as essential elements of Christian mission.

Unfortunately, too much traditional evangelical missionary effort and activity has had the character of a crusade. It has had an aggressive and even implicitly arrogant approach which has explicitly depended on military violence of the Christian West to underwrite and protect it. For example, the Christian and Missionary Alliance missionaries in Vietnam during the war identified with the American armed forces and formally called their United States churches to prayer for an American success. The Area Secretary for South East Asia wrote, "I cannot believe that it is in God's providence or purpose that an additional fifty-six million people be sealed off from free access to the message of the gospel."[1]

Still more recently the "peace position," as Mennonites often refer to it, has become identified with active peacemaking. During the 1960s and 1970s, some Mennonites were actively involved in the civil rights conflict and began to speak of nonviolence and non-cooperation instead of nonresistance and nonconformity, the latter having been the old separatist vocabulary. We began to recognize *systemic* violence and to join in nonviolent protest of injustice. Then during the Vietnam War some Mennonite young men opposed the war by refusing to register for the draft. Others refused to pay the portion of taxes that would be used to finance war and instead sent it to peace causes.

Mennonites began to see that there really can be no true peace without justice. Still more recently, while peace and justice projects in the areas of racial conflict and economic injustice continue, our attention has turned to peace building through mediation and conflict transformation. The pacifism that Jesus taught involves us in active peacemaking, not passive nonresistance. It requires proactive involvement to establish justice and transform conflict, not reactive social withdrawal to preserve moral purity; and calls us to active protest and non-cooperation with violence and social evil, not private objection and quiet submission to the status quo.

While I do not intend to discuss here the pros and cons of the classical just war theory, I do want to recognize it as a significant step on the continuum from the justification of violence as a political means, on the one hand, to the rejection of all violence on the other. There is a qualitative distance between the advocacy of violence as a redemptive means in the Christian cause and the reluctant limited use of coercive force to restrain evil. It is one thing to identify soldiers who died in military combat killing for the political causes of Christian civilization as martyrs. As I understand it, this is what leaders like Ian Paisley, the Orange Order, Jerry Falwell, and Pat Robertson do. And it is quite another to place the church on the side of nonviolence yet recognize the dilemma that exists in a violent world, as the statement of the General Assembly of the Presbyterian Church in Northern Ireland does in its 1994 statement, the "Peace Vocation" of the church.

Reflections on the Argument for Nonviolence

Observations

Building on this brief overview of Mennonite experience, I want first to share some observations on the nature of the argument for nonviolence when we shift from a focus on nonresistance and pacifism to nonviolence. Nonresistance generally focuses the issue on how we should respond in a crisis when our fellows or we are threatened by immediate physical vio lence as in the time of war. The discussion of *non*violence implicitly assumes that we are operating in the context of violence, and the specific question being addressed is how to challenge systemic violence and break the circle of overt violence.

The theory of nonviolence rejects what Walter Wink calls the "myth of redemptive violence"—that the social order is ontologically based on violence. Christian nonviolence challenges the claim that in the name of Jesus Christ his followers are ever justified in countering violence with violent response. I do not think we are debating whether all forms of coercive restraint or discipline are forbidden. Rather, how in the spirit of Jesus the violence so rampant and taken for granted in our world can be overcome.

Approaching the subject this way requires a clear definition of violence. The word *violence* comes from the Latin *violentus* and has several different meanings. Some of them have no moral implication. It may mean simply a swift intense physical force; but it also may signify unjust, disrespectful or irreverent action against the law, or causing harm or damage to a person. To *violate* comes also from this same root—*violatus*, to treat with violence, to assault as in rape. I do not assume that all coercive force is an act of moral violence. For the purpose of evaluating the ethical legitimacy of physical coercion, violence is that which violates the essential humanity, or personal selfhood, of a fellow human being. In theological terms it is an action that rejects/denies (demonizes) and violates (assaults) one made in the "image of God." It is that which dehumanizes the other person, whether friend or enemy.

Building a logical case based on biblical texts cannot make the argument for Christian nonviolence. The same, of course, can also be said for a literalistic approach to justifying the death penalty (legalized violence). The power of the argument to convince lies in the character and example of Jesus, and its sanction has a paradigmatic quality, not the demonstrative quality of linear logic. Further, by the very nature of the case the application of nonviolence in any and every specific situation will need to be contextual. Its moral validity in each case depends on the situation and the attitudes of those involved. That is most likely the reason why Jesus' instructions deal with the inner motivation, not the letter of the law.

Pacifism and Nonviolence

The societal context and cultural presuppositions in which the case for or against pacifism has been argued have changed substantially over the past one hundred years. Arguing for nonviolence is not the same as advocating a particular version of pacifism or nonresistance, and vice-versa. The case for each of the positions will be construed somewhat differently although they may overlap. Martin Luther King Jr., for example, whose influence had much to do with the shift of the argument from nonresistance to pacifism and nonviolent resistance, was pacifist. Miroslav Volf, a Croatian free church theologian, in his *Exclusion and Embrace*, makes a cultural analyses and biblical argument for a consistent Christian nonviolence with a strong bias for biblical pacifism. Walter Wink, in *Engaging the Powers*, seems to be both nonviolent and pacifist in a postmodernist perspective. John Howard Yoder, a Mennonite theologian best known for his *Politics of Jesus*, made a strong case following World War II for the more traditional biblical nonresistance.

Arguing for any of these positions requires and presumes a theological paradigm which provides its supporting context. But within the Western Augustinian tradition, the controlling hermeneutical paradigm already rejects nonviolence as a realistic social ethic. It assumes that the church, the City of God, exists as a spiritual reality/kingdom amid a sinful earthly "City of Man" in which violence is not only inevitable but necessary to maintain God's just will. Thus, as a supernatural spiritual institution existing "between the times," the church must cooperate with the governing powers in executing violence to maintain justice and defeat evil. Thus the temporal existence of the church has been spiritualized and institutionalized and the "kingdom" ethic of Jesus postponed to the eschaton for fulfillment.

Protestantism adopted and adapted the Augustinian and Thomistic paradigm of two kingdoms, a temporal and a spiritual, to construct a theological ethic for Christians in the political world. Anabaptists, children of the Reformation, argued the *nonresistance position* from the hermeneutical presuppositions of this Protestant orthodoxy at the same time as they challenged a number of its Augustinian presuppositions. The *pacifist position* has generally been argued from liberal Protestant presuppositions that assume a post-millennial paradigm. And the *nonviolent position*, where it takes itself seriously as more than a tactical social process, must come to terms with many of the profound theological issues in Christianity no matter which species (feminist, biblicist, pragmatist) it represents. Miraslov Volf is a good example of one who wrestles with the biblical witness. He speaks out of the extreme violence of Bosnia-Croatia as a conservative Christian who is not from a nonresistant or nonviolent tradition.

I have concluded that a theological ethic of nonviolence, what Mennonites call a peace theology, is at a decided disadvantage when it accepts the traditional theological paradigm of Protestant orthodoxy as its originating context. Mennonites have tended to assume that evangelical theology is correct in the essentials, and that it only needs the corrective of a more New Testament concept of peacemaking. In fact, however, a bias for the necessity of remedial or redemptive violence is built into the methodological presuppositions of orthodoxy.

I argue that the almost five hundred-year Reformed Anabaptist debate about pacifism has been largely unproductive for the same reasons and in the same manner that the Liberal-Fundamentalist debate has ended in a standoff. And I might add that the two hundred-year battles between conservative and liberal Protestants, presumably to make some fundamental corrections in the Protestant system, only exacerbated the hermeneutical situation in the debate about nonviolence. Conservative leaders in the United States often criticized Mennonites as "liberal," and Liberals counted them as another fundamentalist sect. Reinhold Niebuhr allowed them the ethical legitimacy of a vocational position in light of the nature of the issue, and spoke of them as the conscience of Protestants. Arguably the Mennonite inconsistency stemming from its appropriation of Protestant theological categories, while quite understandable, is largely responsibility for this confusion.

A theological rational for a nonviolent Christianity will have to begin at the beginning to analyze the biblical perspective—what Karl Barth called "the strange, new world within the Bible." It will need to reevaluate the governing emphasis of evangelicalism on justification with its ethical ramifications, and in its place make reconciliation and transformation the controlling paradigm. The act that is at the center of the evangelical doctrine of justification is an act of "just vengeance," and it becomes the Christian rationale for demanding violent penal justice in the Christian social order. Retributive punishment is necessary to uphold the moral imperative of divine law. Not deterrence or reformation but painful violent suffering to match the heinousness of the sin![2]

I hasten to add that this in no sense need imply deemphasizing salvation by grace, which is the true center of the gospel. It will, however, involve a reinterpretation of Jesus as the "pioneer and perfecter of our faith" and not simply as the divine sacrifice paying the penalty for the sins of the world. And it will need to re-examine the vocation of the church as the body and sacrament of Christ in the world. What does it mean for the church to be the authentic representative of the one who refused to retaliate, and who's one consistent command to his followers was to "take up their cross and follow his example?"

Understanding Jesus' Mission and the Imperative of Nonviolence

Understanding the implications of Jesus' call to nonviolence/peace is not simply a matter of comparing certain texts from his teachings or relating them to the old covenant, although of course it does include that. One must seek to understand his teaching in the context of his life and mission. What was his vocation as the the Messiah? How is his messianic vocation related to the vocation of individual disciples and the church? How does his nonviolent life pattern relate to the church?

Jesus did not come for the purpose of dying, as is so often said in evangelical circles. He accepted the calling to be the Messiah despite the inevitability of a martyr death, which he seems to have been aware of from the beginning. He came to introduce the kingdom of God, not to suffer a metaphysical punishment that would somehow balance the moral debt of humankind. In the latter case punishment means more than discipline, more than suffering the inherent consequences of sinful action. It is an act of violence which will "satisfy" infinite vengeance, or wrath, which we defend as justice according to the law of "eye for eye and tooth for tooth." Viewed from this perspective, the focus shifts from the necessity of a violent punitive death demanded by a God who "must punish sin."

This shift of focus removes the implicit justification for punitive violence from the center of the hermeneutics of atonement theory. At the same time it helps to explain the language of conflict and struggle which so characterizes the accounts of Jesus' ministry. It points to the actual purpose of his nonviolent public ministry, which was in no sense passive. Indeed, it was what gave meaning to his supreme act of nonviolence on the cross. As Volf puts it,

> Active opposition to the kingdom of Satan, the kingdom of deception and oppression, is therefore inseparable from the proclamation of the kingdom of God. It is this opposition that brought Christ Jesus to the cross; and it is this opposition that gave meaning to his nonviolence. It takes the struggle against deception and oppression to transform nonviolence from barren negativity into creative possibility, from quicksand into a foundation of a new world.[3]

As his disciples understood it, the cross and resurrection were at the center of Jesus' mission, and the gospel writers present his whole ministry as bearing the cross. His ministry is, as it were, the overture to the Passion. The cross and resurrection define the pattern of Jesus' life, and disciples were commanded to imitate this pattern. John Yoder,[4] followed by Miroslav Volf, noted that the only specific thing that Jesus explicitly commanded us to imitate in his lifestyle is taking up the cross. The cross, which is the climactic expression of Jesus' nonviolence, is the ultimate expression of obedience and trust (faithfulness), and the resurrection is the validation of Jesus' understanding of God's will and vindication of his trust.

The kingdom of God is at the heart of Jesus' message and mission, and at the heart of the kingdom of God is the law of non-retaliation. Mathew 5:38-48 is of profound importance for understanding the character of the kingdom, and its significance has not been generally understood. In that text Jesus explicitly says that he is changing the law governing the response to violence in the kingdom of God from the old rule of Torah that limited just retaliation to an equal revenge—"eye for an eye and a tooth for a tooth." The new law of the kingdom he is introducing is one of strict non-retaliation. The point is not non*resistance*, i.e., to remain passive in the face of "evil" or do nothing to rectify the evil that has been done. The point is that what is done to rectify the evil shall not be retaliatory or vengeful. But it does require a resolution. The achievement of God's justice requires a nonviolent solution that puts reconciliation and transformation ahead of one that achieves legal justice by settling the score. "Blessed are the peacemakers."

The Vocation of the Church

This brings us to the calling of the church as the continuing sacramental presence of Christ in the world. It is the vocation of the church as the body of Christ, not of one denomination within the institutional body as Reinhold Niebuhr maintained, to continue Jesus' witness to the kingdom of God as a nonviolent possibility in the world.

In his instruction to Christian slaves, Peter is very clear that the cross (the essential symbol of Christ's nonviolence) is an example for Christians to follow (1 Pet. 2: 11-25). According to the apostle Paul, death and resurrection establish a new paradigm for Christian living. In the letter to Colossians, Paul speaks of his own imprisonment as "completing in his own body what is lacking in Christ's afflictions for the sake of the body" (1:24). According to Philippians 3:10-11, "knowing Christ" meant "becoming like him in his death, if somehow I may attain the resurrection from the dead." The cross becomes the symbol of the believer's imitation of Christ's suffering, i.e. nonviolent lifestyle, in the hope of resurrection and God's ultimate victory.

And this is not merely a spiritual exercise for individual Christians. The church as the body of Christ shares in the continuation of Christ's salvation ministry in a way that necessitates its imitation of his lifestyle. The church is the present manifestation of the rule of God and shares the vocation of the Christ to introduce the kingdom. As his body, it is the "fullness of him [the risen Christ] who fills all in all" (Eph. 2:22-23). Its mission is reconciliation and peace making between humans and between humans and God (Eph. 2:14). Nonviolent redemptive action is the vocation of the church as it participates in the mission of God.

Notes

1. See my *Community of the Spirit* (Scottdale, Pa.: Herald Press, 1993), 198, n. 7.

2. See Timothy Gorringe, *God's Just Vengeance: Crime, Violence, and the Rhetoric of Salvation* (Cambridge: Cambridge University Press, 1996), 200ff.

3. *Exclusion and Embrace: A Theological Exploration of identity, Otherness, and Reconciliation* (Nashville: Abingdon Press, 1996) 293.

4. Yoder's works are voluminous, but his most popular and well-known work is *The Politics of Jesus* (Grand Rapids: Eerdmans, 1975).

5

Jesus and the Politics of Peace

An Overview of the Problem

In his epilogue to *The Historical Jesus,* John Dominic Crossan raises the persistent question whether "an understanding of the historical Jesus [is] of any permanent relevance to Christianity itself." And he continues to answer his own question: "I think, therefore, that different visions of the historical Jesus present a certain dialectic with different theological interpretations and that the New Testament itself is an obvious expression of that plurality's inevitability." I would only emphasize that the obvious plurality of interpretations has for its subject the one human person located in a historical time and place. Thus, as Crossan himself puts it deftly, our Christianity is and will always be a "Jesus/Christ/ianity."[1]

It is my contention that a contemporary *anabaptist* reading of the Gospels is one such authentic theological perspective. It represents what Crossan in a later book refers to as "an evangelical layer" of the gospel text, [2] and while not strictly speaking scientific history, it is an authentic reflection of the essential message and character of the real Jesus. Thus the Jesus who "endured the cross" will always be the one "on whom [our] faith depends from start to finish" (Heb. 12:2 NEB).

Luther and Protestantism in general made a sharp distinction between the vocation of Jesus as divine Messiah and the vocation, or calling, of his disciples. Luther followed the medieval template of temporal and spiritual callings, which distinguished between the religious (church) and political (state) vocations. The Messiah's vocation to be our savior and suffer for the sins of the world necessitated a distinct life style and separation from the world of power politics. His was a spiritual calling which required a unique social and political stance. Therefore, his teachings and example are not to be understood as a pattern for human society. They are to be spiritualized and applied to individual personal attitudes and actions. But at the same time, disciples must live as citizens of the old order obeying the laws of the state and recognizing its authority to require participation in its violent coercive action.

Anabaptists, on the other hand, insisted that disciples are to follow the example and teachings of Jesus in every aspect of life, both temporal and spiritual, secular and religious. As citizens of heaven under the lordship of Christ, they participate in his mission of bearing witness to the kingdom of God (see 1 Pet. 2; Phil. 3; Rom. 12-13; Eph. 2:17-22). Obviously this raised many issues demanding ethical and theological discrimination, and sixteenth-century Anabaptist leaders did not always agree with each other (e.g., Balthasar Hubmaier versus Menno Simons). They often attempted to resolve these questions by literalistic appeals, some of which we might consider inappropriate, to the texts of Scripture. Nevertheless, the basic theological divergence between Protestant and Anabaptist understandings of Jesus' political significance remain unresolved and call for continuing discernment.

Understanding the first-century context is comparatively easy. Learning and translating the languages, studying the historical context, comparing synoptic texts—all that must go into a scholarly exegesis—can produce a relatively acceptable interpretation. The larger problem arises when we try to make cross-cultural transfers from the first to the twenty-first century cultures. What are the political implications of Jesus for our age of nuclear threats, terror, and war? How do we authentically apply the practice and spirit of Jesus' political significance?[3]

More than a simple word study and exegesis of New Testament texts are required to make an authentic cross-cultural transfer. One must do more than extract certain sayings from Jesus' teachings and reconcile them with the Mosaic covenant, although of course the transfer does include that. One must do an evaluative analysis of our contemporary cultures. Interpreting and applying his teachings to our contemporary age requires a theological as well as a grammatical-historical reading of the texts and a transcultural contextualization of their content.

The first step in this theological contextualization involves understanding the teaching of Jesus in the context of his messianic vocation, then relating his messianic vocation to the vocation of individual disciples and the church. How does Jesus' nonviolent life pattern relate to the mission of the church? The second task in the interpretative process requires cross-cultural contextualization. Much has changed in the cultural and societal landscape over two millennia. The New Testament's first-century commandments to live a nonviolent lifestyle have to be adapted to our social and political structures and presuppositions.

Merely quoting biblical texts cannot adequately answer such questions. They require sensitive cultural analysis, spiritual and theological perception, and moral discernment. It is not the immediate purpose of this chapter to elaborate a moral political ethic or an alternative nonviolent political strategy. Others have been and are working at that task. The more limited purpose is to develop a theological hermeneutic to support nonviolent involvement in the political quest for justice.

The Political Role of the Messiah

Put in theological terms, raising the question of Jesus' political significance is simply asking how the atonement, accomplished in the cross and resurrection, impacts the sociopolitical realm. And to do that one must understand the social gestalt as well as the ontological nature of the "Messiah." It assumes that his life and teaching were not focused only on inner spirituality with heaven as a goal. He came as the Reconciler—the Mediator between God and humanity, and between alienated human factions (Eph. 2:11-14). He came offering God's *shalom* (peace) to the nations—God's "will on *earth* as it is in heaven."

The Gospels present Jesus as the true fulfillment of the Mosaic covenant which defined Israel as God's holy nation (Exod. 19:6). Too often our theological language of "law and grace" fails to recognize the significance of Jesus' words, "Do not think that I have come to abolish the law or the prophets; I have come not to abolish but to fulfill" (Matt. 5:17). While this is not the place for a detailed analysis of Jesus' relation to Moses and the prophets, we do need to establish the cultural religious context for interpreting his life and teaching.

Protestantism in both its present evangelical wing as well as an earlier liberal version[4] imaged the kingdom as an individual and spiritual reality. But as James Charlesworth points out, when Jesus' message is understood in its first-century Hebraic context, such dichtomoy is unlikely. He writes, "God's kingdom is not exclusively individualistic, a society in the human heart (a *societas cordibus*). In one sense, Jesus could not establish something so completely unprecedented, because he inherited ancient Jewish traditions and spoke to Israel, a nation constituted and carried on by God's historical acts."[5] Jesus as the Messiah ("Son of God") fulfilled Israel's duty under the Mosaic covenant and called the people to a new obedience as God's beloved people (Matt. 5:17-20).

Into this ancient cultural and religious setting Jesus, a Jewish messianic figure, came preaching the kingdom of God. He offered himself as the prophetic pioneer and messianic leader of the kingdom. He blessed the "peacemakers" and those who "hunger and thirst for justice. He taught his disciples to pray that God's authority would be recognized on earth as it is in heaven." N. T. Wright, following in the tradition of John Howard Yoder's *Politics of Jesus*, puts it simply: Jesus was "offering an alternative politics."[6]

According to the Mosaic covenant, Israel was called to be the special "people of God." God was their king, and their vocation among the nations was to advance their King's authority and rule in the earth. They were to imitate Yahweh ("to be holy as God was holy"); to be a people of God's shalom on earth demonstrating an alternative politics to the nations around them. Their constitution and laws were spelled out in the Torah (Law), and expanded on by the prophets who contextualized them in the following centuries.[7]

In Jesus' day the scribes (lawyers) and Pharisees assumed the role of interpreting and applying the sacred text. They thought of themselves as "guides" (Matt. 15:14; 23:16; Rom. 2:19) to the nation interpreting the will of God on earth. They were the purveyors of the wisdom of the Torah guiding the national political ethos. By the first century A. D. the Mosaic Torah was viewed as the revealed source of God's wisdom, and they were moral casuists applying the Mosaic legal tradition to the everyday life.[8]

In the later words of the apostle Paul, who had been one of them, they were very zealous for the Law of Moses, and they hued to the literal application of the text as much as possible. They did not think of themselves as prophets. They were biblical exegetes and approached the Mosaic text as a legal document. For example, they dealt with the command to do no work on the Sabbath by analyzing the nature of "work" and defining the precise time the Sabbath begins.

Into this scenario enters John the Baptist, not in scribal guise but in a prophetic role. Jesus called him the last and greatest in the prophetic tradition. His criticism of the contemporary Jewish political establishment called for a genuine moral response to Torah, which his exhortation to the multitudes sums up in sociopolitical requirements. His ethical teaching recapitulates the best of the Law and the prophets and points beyond itself to the eschatological fulfillment of the Mosaic covenant.[9]

The Baptist himself expected Jesus to go even farther in the establishment of the new order (Matt. 11:3; Luke 7:18-20). According to both Matthew and Luke, he had messianic expectations for Jesus, which he cast in the prophetic mold of his own calling. He expected Jesus to be more powerful and to baptize with the Spirit (Luke 3:16-17). Jesus as the messianic prophet would reestablish God's kingship on earth by renewing and restoring Israel as God's people. This would include a more thorough judgment and coercive purging of evil, followed by a reign of peace and justice.

But Jesus did not follow John's prophetic role model! If he saw himself as messiah, it was not as a prophet of judgment threatening violent punishment. His mission was not to pronounce more severe judgment and the eradication of evil by coercion but rather to heal, reconcile, and overcome evil with good (Luke 7:18-23). He was no Amos redividus thundering at a corrupt priesthood and the "cows of Bashan." Nor was he an Elijah tilting with Ahab and slaying the prophets of Baal (1 Kings 18:44f.). If he is to be framed in a prophetic role, it must be more like the "holy man of God" Elisha, who followed Elijah (2 Kings 4:9).

In the words of Ben Witherington, Jesus seems clearly to have assumed the style of a "prophetic sage"[10]—a teacher and practitioner of wisdom, in the tradition of late Judaism. As such he engaged in a sharp critique of scribal hermeneutics and in the announcement of a more spiritual understanding of the intention and eschatological goal of the Mosaic Law. Although the modifier *prophetic* must be maintained in contrast to the scribal casuistical tradition, Jesus took the posture of a sage. He did not present himself as a prophetic oracle. He came teaching an alternative wisdom to that of the scribes and Pharisees.

His teachings should be understood and interpreted in this semantic mode.[11] He made use of aphorisms, of which, Marcus Borg reminds us, there are more than one hundred,[12] to advocate a point of view. He presented some of his most profound and radical teachings in parables. To him wisdom is not ontological speculation as in the Neoplatonic writers but a matter of godly prudence. His instruction is offered as an alternative way of life which will be vindicated in the living of it (Luke 7:31).

This is set over against the traditional wisdom of the elders, which presents social reality as viewed by current Judaism. For example, Jesus clearly rejects the notion of "redemptive violence" that was at the very heart of conventional morality (Matt. 5:38-39). Jesus' commands are not so much legislative prescriptions as they are statements of the true nature of human society and relationships and call for a transformation (*metanonia*) of one's life patterns.

Jesus initiated a renewal movement that called Israel to a new and different interpretation of the Mosaic Law. As we shall see, he did not reject the Torah as an authoritative guide to the regulation of society under the kingship of Yahweh. Rather he offered a different interpretation of its intention in light of his understanding of the character of God. Jesus called for a sociopolitical response based upon religious, or spiritual, convictions about God and God's will for Israel. He was not simply a mystic and sage drawing spiritual lessons for individuals. He formed a movement, and his movement—in contrast to the Pharisees, Essenes, and Zealots—called for a consistent nonviolent response to conflict, both among themselves and with Rome.

He accepted the calling to be a nonviolent messiah despite the inevitability of a martyr death, which he seems to have been aware of from the beginning. He did not come for the purpose of dying, as it is often said in evangelical circles. He came to introduce the kingdom of God, not to suffer a metaphysical punishment that would somehow balance the moral debt of humankind. As he struggled to understand the meaning of his calling, he became convinced that it was to conform to the pattern of the Suffering Servant pictured in Isaiah 42:1-4. And he held steadfastly to that vision even thought it meant the inevitability of his execution.

Jesus' Relation to John the Baptist

The relation of Jesus' teaching to the Old Testament text has long been a subject of controversy in the Protestant world. Is the Sermon on the Mount to be understood as a radical reversal of the Mosaic tradition that allowed, indeed commanded, retaliation, war, and the death penalty? Or does it assume and confirm it for political purposes, and make Jesus' own pattern an individual or personal response to evil? What relevance does Jesus' teaching on non-retaliation have for the political order? Clearly John the Baptist is a bridge character, and his relation to Jesus provides a clue to the answer of these questions.

The relation of John the Baptist and his ministry to Jesus' ministry has a hermeneutical bearing on the way in which Jesus' teachings are to be understood. Although John and Jesus are linked together in the "beginning of the gospel" (Mark 1:1ff), there are obvious differences in their style and the content of ministry and teaching. Both Matthew and Luke call attention to these differences by including the story of John's questions to Jesus from his prison cell (Matt.11: 2-19; Luke 7:18-25).

These differences pertain to both style and the eschatological relation of John to the kingdom of God. Does John as the last in the prophetic tradition introduce the rule of God but not enter it? Or is he the herald and trailblazer who is included as the harbinger of what is to follow? Is his advice to the "crowds" that came to hear him (Luke 3:10-14) to be understood as an assumed base for understanding the thrust of Jesus' teachings on nonviolence? Or is it to be considered part of the tradition of the elders preceding Jesus, which Jesus' teachings superceded?

There is clearly a difference in their styles of ministry. Ben Witherington III has accounted for this by noting that John stands in the tradition of the classical Hebrew prophets and Jesus "came across as a prophetic and eschatological sage." [13] I am persuaded with many contemporary Jesus scholars that this is correct, and that the difference between a Lawgiver or classical prophet, and sage or teacher of wisdom must influence how we interpret and use Jesus' ethical instruction in our contemporary society.

For example, if his teachings in the Sermon on the Mount are read as wisdom sayings, they should not be interpreted and used as a new *law* with its commandments and taboos, but as a "pattern for life," to use the title of A. H. Hunter's classic exposition of the Sermon.[14] They have the character of wisdom sayings given on various occasions, and probably many times over, for instruction in "the Christian way."[15] They should not be understood and used as the legal parallel of the dogmas and theological creeds drawn up in the following centuries. This stylistic difference does have implications for the application of Jesus' teaching in cross-cultural settings, but does it alone explain the contrast in the approach and messages of the two men?

The theological implications of the Baptist's relation to the kingdom of God, which is the focus of Jesus' mission, is more crucial to the hermeneutical task of understanding and applying Jesus' sayings to our modern political situation. In his *Theology of St. Luke,* Hans Conzelmann points out that Matthew and Mark consider John to be the first act in the ensuing drama as the forerunner of the Messiah. Mark's Gospel announces the beginning of the "good news of Jesus Christ" by introducing John (1:1-4), and Matthew presents him as the "Elijah" predicted to come as the harbinger of the Messiah (11:13-14). In Luke, on the other hand, John is portrayed as the last of the prophets, and as such he represents the end of the pre-Jesus salvation story. In Conzelmann's words, Luke does not think that John's appearance is "an eschatological event."[16]

This is hermeneutically significant for interpreting the marked differences between the teachings of John and Jesus. If John simply marks the end of the old dispensation in a historical sequence of activity, then we may assume that his advice to the multitudes is to be considered part of the tradition of the ancestors to which Jesus' teaching is contrasted. If he is the eschatological introduction to and included in the new dispensation of the gospel, then we must assume that his advice provides the semantic context for understanding Jesus' teaching on violence.

Clearly the two figures, John and Jesus, overlap. By insisting that John should baptize him "to fulfill all righteousness" (Matt. 3:15) Jesus recognizes John as an authentic prophet and allies himself with his mission. According to Matthew, he seems to reduce the difference between himself and John to one of style—ascetic prophet versus popular sage (11:16-19). He praises John as "more than a prophet" and acknowledges his preparatory role in introducing the kingdom of God. Further, Jesus continues John's call to Israel to repent, and warns of impending doom if they refused. He too warns of violent and destructive consequences in "outer darkness" and a "*Gehenna* of fire" for those who do not repent. And as if to introduce his challenge to scribal interpretations of the Torah (Matt. 5:22ff) he announces that he has not come to abolish the law and the prophets, which John represented (5:17). Thus, as Charlesworth points out, Jesus accepts a "possible rival" as a significant part of his own mission.[17]

On the other hand, John clearly represents the priestly tradition of Law. His advice to the crowds does not go beyond the current interpretation of the prophetic and wisdom writings. His advice to the soldiers may be taken to discourage revolt (Luke 3:14), but it clearly assumes the use of coercive force to regulate society. He does not challenge the traditional hierarchical society based on inherited social status, shame and honor as social sanctions, and justice defined by the Mosaic formula, "an eye for an eye." Thus, Luke's observation in 16:16 that "the law and the prophets were in effect until John came; since then the good news of the kingdom of God is proclaimed" would seem fully justified.

In what may be a further contrast of the style and substance of John and Jesus, both Luke and Matthew comment that "from the days of John the Baptist until now the kingdom of heaven has suffered violence, and the violent take it by force" (Matt. 11:12). This obscure saying has been variously interpreted. Elaborating on a suggestion made by T. W. Manson many years ago,[18] I suggest that at least it implies that John's preaching did not change the basic assumptions about the role of coercive violence in establishing the kingdom of God, and that, according to Matthew, Jesus' ministry introduced a nonviolent approach.[19]

Traditional nonresistant interpretations of the Sermon on the Mount have generally assumed that John belonged to the old dispensation, and that his exhortations to the multitudes recorded in Luke 3:10-14, which presuppose and condone the coercive regulation of society, have no application to the kingdom of God. They assume that Jesus' teaching of nonresistant love and forgiveness of "enemies" replaces them as the new law of the kingdom. In a word, Jesus' ethic has been understood in contrast to John's as a counsel of absolute nonresistance to evil (bearing the cross), and not as an ethic of peacemaking and nonviolent resistance to evil.[20] But if we assume that John's exhortations establish the sociopolitical context for understanding Jesus' teaching, a new way of reading it becomes plausible.

Jesus, Coercion, and Violence

Israel deeply resented Roman domination, which it considered both a political and a religious indignity. The Pharisees, Zealots, and Essenes were all in favor of violent resistance to maintain the religio-political integrity of Israel, although they differed about political strategies.[21] Into this potentially violent situation, John introduced Jesus as a messianic savior, i.e., a savior of the nation. John clearly expected him to assume the role of a prophetic political leader, but Jesus did not follow that path, as we have seen. Rather he adopted the identity of a peripatetic rabbi and sage. He was recognized as a charismatic teacher and healer. His sayings were primarily religious advocating a pattern of life, but in first-century Judaism one cannot separate religion and politics.

This is the contextual setting in which the Jewish Messiah, Jesus, and his teachings must be situated. Following the path opened by John the Baptizer, who represented the highest political and religious morality of the Hebrew prophets, Jesus taught an alternative interpretation of the Mosaic Torah, which he claimed would actually fulfill its true meaning and usher in the "kingdom of God." He did not abolish the Law and the prophets but offered Israel a way to authentically fulfill its vocation as God's people. This being the case, it is crucial to understand what the crux of the difference was between the conservative Jewish leaders and Jesus' new teaching.

Jesus' words, "You have heard that it was said to those of ancient times . . . But I say to you . . ." (Matt. 5:21) should not be understood as the abolition of the law or the prophets, but as their fulfillment (Matt. 5:17-20). The good news was not that the Mosaic Law had been revoked, but rather that its legal application based upon a literalistic hermeneutic had been transcended.

This point is important for our understanding of Jesus' assumptions and attitude toward coercive action. His teachings about the kingdom of God build on the salvation message of the prophets; they do not displace it. The good news is not that God, who heaped the ontological consequences of sinful (violent) action upon Christ, now indulges sinners. The system of moral coercion implicit in creation has not been eradicated. Such coercive action is inherent in the human social structure and plays its role limiting the consequences of evil.[22]

One can only assume that John the Baptist agreed in general with the pharisaic ethic and was critical only of of its superficial and inconsistent practice. His admonitions to the public, as we have seen, stay well within the limitations of organized society. To the crowds who ask, "What shall we do?" he advocates generosity and mutuality, but he does not challenge private property. He exhorts the tax collectors to honesty and fair assessment. (Compare Zacchaeus in Luke 19: 8.) He tells the "soldiers," which probably includes police, not to misuse their position and power for self-serving advantage. They are neither to extort money by physical intimidation from those they police nor to rebel against the system that hired them. They are to play by the rules of a just society and to restrain their coercion within the limits of a just social order.

While Jesus in both style and substance differs from the Baptist, he seems to have assumed that coercive government implied in John's exhortation is a legitimate aspect of the created social order. He does not teach that government is the result of human depravity although its task has certainly been affected by the Fall.[23] Therefore, government is not sinful or evil in itself, although it operates in an imperfect society with an imperfect instrument—namely, law—and Jesus has come to call people to a voluntary obedience of law that makes violent coercion unnecessary (Matt. 5:20).

Jesus counseled his disciples to "give to Caesar what belongs to Caesar," to pay their taxes and obey the regulations of a governing elite to maintain order in society. He did not advocate rebellion against the occupying power of Rome, as did the Zealots and the Pharisees. When he observed that "they who take the sword will perish with the sword," he gave pragmatic recognition to the fact that those who live according to the minimal mandates and sanctions of the law must expect coercive consequences. Or again as a bit of pragmatic wisdom he advised his followers to be reconciled with their accusers before they were taken to court, and he warned that if they were found guilty they would suffer the full sentence. I cite these as examples of his compliant attitude toward the social mores and legal prescriptions of society that imply coercive regulation.

On the other hand, he nowhere condones the use of violence. He does not ground coercive violence in the nature and action of God, whom, he taught, distributes blessings on humankind indiscriminately. He does, however, teach that there are ontological consequences built into people's behavior. He warns of "hell-fire" and "outer darkness" as the result of sinful action—certainly a coercive constraint of evil! But we must note that in the shame culture of which he was part, hell was not necessarily a violent deterrent used to coerce people into right conduct! Rather, as the original word *Gehenna* suggests, hell is the rubbish heap of the universe where the despicable and self-destroying miscreants are disposed of. Hell is a kind of intrinsic result, not an assigned extrinsic punishment. It results from the inherent consequences of the actions themselves. Hell is a kind of purgation of the "unclean," unholy, and evil pollution, not a vindictive punishment.

This raises the question whether *nonviolent* coercive restraint of evil, including physical restraint short of doing lethal harm, plays any legitimate role in the ethical pattern of Jesus' life and teaching. Granted that there is no justification for recourse to retaliatory violence, is there a place for coercive restraint of violent action?[24] Does an ethic of agape allow, or perhaps even dictate, nonviolent resistance to systemic, exploitative evil in the social order? To these and similar questions the traditional ethic of nonresistance has generally replied in the negative, but there are hermeneutical reasons to question whether Jesus' life and teaching support this reply.

The words *coercion* and *violence* overlap in their meanings, and for purposes of moral analysis and evaluation they must be more precisely defined.[25] Both imply the use of force or threat of force against the will of the offender, but violence also carries the meaning of its cognate "to violate" (*violatus*) which comes from the same root. In this sense it indicates action against people that debases, assaults as in rape, or destroys in hostile or unjust action. It is in this sense that Jesus' sayings against all violence are to be understood.

This, of course, does not speak to the moral dilemma of intervening with potentially lethal coercive force when physical violence immediately threatens the destruction of self and others. But in contrast to absolute pacifism or nonresistance, the violence/coercion distinction suggests the need for more nuanced moral discrimination in situations that call for coercive engagement to maintain social order. The distinction recognizes the legitimacy of law, which by its very nature is coercive. The distinction allows substituting the law of love, which may include the use of coercive restraint, for the law of retribution, or vengeful coercion. Indeed, it defines the latter as *violence*. Love is not understood as passive or indulgent response to destructive action, but as empathetic respect for, and genuine desire for the welfare of the other person. The distinction leaves open the question whether agape might in an extreme case require potentially lethal coercive action.[26]

Walter Wink has suggested an innovative and morally attractive resolution to the impasse created by absolute nonresistance.[27] He equates violence with evil and attempts to make the case for nonviolent coercion (p. 192). Wink assumes that the focus of Jesus' concern is on the evil of violent force and suggests that Jesus presents a "third way" that seizes the moral initiative and finds a creative alternative to violence. One should not "react violently to evil, do not counter evil in kind" (p. 186). This becomes the basis for determining the legitimacy of "nonviolent" resistance to injustice. Moral conversion by persuasion, and if necessary by coercion, is allowable, but "*violent* coercion" (italics his) may not be employed (p. 192).[28]

Wink quotes Barbara Deming's characterization of this nonviolent use of force to persuade the opponent even against his/her will. In her essay, "On Revolution and Equilibrium," Deming writes that in nonviolent action one "exerts force upon the other, not tearing him away from himself but tearing from him only that which is not properly his own, the strength which has been loaned to him by all those who have been giving him obedience" (p. 192). Wink adds also that we should not equate nonviolence with non-conflict. While this is a persuasive contemporary analysis of what may be considered the "good," one cannot point to a Jesus saying that parallels it.

One can only assume that Jesus did not renounce the prophetic ethic of justice summed up in Micah 6:8 or the legal structures of Torah that supported it. He identified with and spoke to the economically and politically powerless multitudes. He did not offer an alternative political structure for either the Jewish power elite or the Roman rulers. His wisdom sayings deal with personal and social inter-dynamics. When he did address the one political option open to the masses, namely violent rebellion, he repudiated violence as an ineffective way to achieve just peace, and, as we shall see, he repudiated vengeance as a measure of justice. This leads us to the crucial text in Matthew 5:38-39.

Jesus and Retributive Justice

The pacifist traditions that have emphasized nonresistance to evil have marshaled their arguments against the moral legitimacy of violence.

Their motto, "Do no violence," focuses on the continuum of violent behavior from nonviolent action to lethal violence in war, and the critical moral issue hinges on self-defense. Defined in its broadest terms, the question is whether lethal violence is justified in the case of self-defense. Dare one even rely on law enforcement agents to defend one's property and oneself? The just war theory is, of course, based on the moral legitimacy of self-defense. And in the international context of the war in Iraq launched by the United States in 2003, the question has been raised whether preemptive violence is justified if it deters greater violence.

In response to the nonviolent philosophy of Gandhi, especially as it was practiced by Martin Luther King in the civil rights movement, Christian ethicists have shifted their attention to the legitimacy of nonviolent resistance. What degree of coercive force is allowable in resistance to injustice? Is nonviolent protest allowed when it threatens economic harm to those who persist in injustice? Can such action be called "doing good" to the enemy? Stated this way, as comparative degrees of violence, the questions do not recognize the crucial moral distinction between coercion and violence in the interpretation of Matthew 5:38-39, where Jesus prohibits retribution as a principle of justice.

The Mosaic Torah defined corrective justice as a balanced equation of belligerently inflicted harm and retributive harm. The operative equation was "an eye for an eye and a tooth for a tooth," which has become the working definition for retributive justice in the so-called Christian West. What we should note in the first place is that according to the Torah justice did not *require* retribution but rather *limited* retribution. Mosaic justice limits retaliation to an equal amount of violence (harm) repaid, but in the casuistry of the Jewish scribes it had virtually become a requirement. Jesus clearly understood this difference and went a step beyond limiting vengeance to equal requital.

Jesus' reinterpretation of the Torah on this point is crucial to an assessment of the political import of his teaching, and Matthew 5:38ff is pivotal to his reinterpretation of the Mosaic Law. It has commonly been translated "do not resist evil," but this wording fails to catch the real thrust of the saying. The Greek word *antistenai* used in the text may be correctly translated "do not resist," but in this context it fails to catch the nuance of meaning. Here Jesus recalls the old definition of justice as an equation of revenge and rejects retaliation as a valid motive or principle of justice altogether.

The Matthew saying does not weigh the comparative legitimacy of violent response but rejects the law of retaliation (*lex talionis*) as the standard of justice. The *Contemporary English Version* has correctly translated the command as "But I tell you not to try to get even with a person who has done something to you."[29] Jesus focuses on the law of retribution that defined ancient tribal justice. It is vengeance and retaliation that mutate coercive force into violence. This gives us a more precise and usable moral barometer to guide us in the resistance of social evil and in peacebuilding.

In the politics of the "Christian" West the same shift from a *limiting* to a *requiring of* retaliation has become the basis of its justice system. The demand for justice by punitive retribution to bring "closure" to acts of violence is little different from that of tribal societies. The observation of an Iraqi police major who said, "We [in Iraq] are an Eastern, tribal society with the principle of vengeance. Revenge will be exacted." differs little in principle from that of the United States or Israel.[30]

Jesus unequivocally rejected this principle! Jesus simply does not indulge in a casuistry of violence. He does not address the question of legitimate coercion to maintain a just stable society. He does repudiate preemptive and terrorist violence partly as ineffective ("Those who take the sword will perish by the sword.") and partly because it is the fruit of anger and vengeance. Vengeance belongs to God alone. Human vengeance is not the response of what we might call ontological justice (righteousness) inherent in the very ground of being. Only the God who blesses both the just and unjust, and can forgive and restore in the very act of judgment, is able to calculate just vengeance.

The human imitation of God in this respect can only be expressed in returning good for evil, but while on the surface what is included in "good" may seem obvious, the politics of good is by no means obvious. Jesus' political wisdom must be understood in the context of his teaching about the kingdom of God and Israel's vocation to demonstrate that kingdom. Israel was to be God's nation consecrated to demonstrating the kind of political order God has ordained. Jesus taught that Israel's God is the God who sends rain and sunshine on friend and foe alike. This God, in the words of 1 John 1:9, is "*just and faithful* to forgive" (italics added)—not indulgent and permissive. And what God requires for citizenship in his kingdom is recognition and imitation of the Father's character in human society. As the *New English Bible* puts it,

"There must be no limit to your goodness, as your heavenly Father's goodness knows no bounds" (Matt. 5:48). Speaking politically, they were to be a kingdom of justice (righteousness) that demonstrated systemic social justice and factored forgiveness into the corrective justice equation.

The Politics of Forgiveness

But is not forgiveness the suspension of political consequences? Is not mercy a kind of indulgence in contrast to justice? In the words of Martha Minow, is not amnesty simply "lawful amnesia"?[31] How can one speak of the politics of forgiveness? What does it mean to factor forgiveness into a political process which is at work to establish both social and retributive justice?

To understand the dynamics of forgiveness as the canceling of retaliatory consequences, we must remember that first-century Jewish society was organized according to a hierarchy of class and privilege where shame and honor were prime motivators. Jesus lived and taught in a shame-oriented culture where settling the score, or, in contemporary terms, "bringing closure," was more a matter of vindicating one's honor than balancing the legal ledger. The gravity of the offense was based on the societal status of the victim. The injured person lost face, and the proper order of relationships in society was disrupted if the offence was ignored. In shame-oriented cultures, acts of retaliation vindicated the *honor* of the one offended. Justice was defined as maintenance of the hierarchical pattern of society, and redress for the violation reestablished the proper order.

Forgiveness was the presumptive right of the superior personage, not of slaves and peasants. Kings and nobles did not need to ask forgiveness of their subjects. Nobles did not owe debts to slaves. Neither did they need to legally justify their acts of moral generosity. Where forgiveness was offered as a gift of generosity, it became a badge of restored honor to the giver, and in itself bespoke the gravity of the offense. The greater the offense forgiven, the more exalted the moral generosity of the one who forgave. Forgiveness as a political act in itself redressed or put right the hierarchical order of society.

Jesus' sayings on forgiveness must first be situated in this context.[32] A quick perusal of the Gospels reveals that there are relatively few references to forgiveness on the lips of Jesus. Nevertheless, his life and example ending with his words from the cross, "Father, forgive them for they know not what they do." make it a commanding theme of his ministry.[33]

His preferred metaphors for forgiveness seem to be the canceling of debt and by implication forgetting the offense. The debts or obligations (*opheilemata*) that need to be forgiven are mistakes or "trespasses" (*paraptomata*), and "sins" (*hamartiai*). Debts are *canceled* (*aphiemi*). And to clear the air trespasses are to be *forgotten*. Sins, understood as general unrighteousness (*adikia*) are viewed as pollution and need to be *cleansed*, or to use a contemporary metaphor, the disk needs to be reformatted.

The full political significance of Jesus' teaching, however, is not to be seen in the metaphors of forgiveness that he used but rather in his egalitarian view of humankind as children of God. He taught that one's true worth as a child of God did not depend on hierarchical social status and that everyone needed and should in turn grant forgiveness. Indeed, no one should expect to receive forgiveness from God, the King of kings, unless they granted it to others (Matt. 6:14-15). Whatever else his prayer to God on the cross might imply, it clearly universalizes this egalitarian perspective.

Forgiveness and Retaliation

Jesus taught that human forgiveness is an act of imitating God by not insisting on one's rights or the vindication of one's honor (Matt. 5:48; 18:27-34). God as King of kings forgives in an act of supreme moral generosity. By virtue of God's righteous power and status, such an act is self-justifying and reestablishes the moral balance of the universe. It does not need extrinsic violent legal requital to give it moral justification. It does not need a sacrificial payment, or penalty, to restore the balance of justice to the moral order. God's magnanimous forgiveness is reflected in the enormity of the debt forgiven, not in the equality of the requital. In a shame-oriented culture, redress focuses on elimination of alienating conflict and the restoration of relationship.

Unfortunately, the implications of this fundamental aspect of God's forgiveness seem to have been lost in contemporary evangelicalism. Operating within a guilt culture, the offense is understood as an affront to law that must be vindicated.[34] Thus forgiveness transmutes into an act of legal indulgence which only God who created the universe can excuse. Sacrifice is interpreted as a symbol of retributive penalty for sin. Especially this is so in orthodox interpretations of the crucifixion of Christ. He is the infinite penalty paid for our sins, thus justifying God's infinite act of indulgence![35]

According to this theological paradigm, forgiveness of societal trespasses becomes an act based on and justified by an action of God that balanced and restored the moral soundness of the universe. According to traditional penal substitutionary theory, even God must satisfy the requirements of retributive justice to be righteous in forgiving humankind. Thus the crucifixion of Christ becomes the justification for a politics of retributive justice, which continues to insist on the death penalty as a moral necessity in the guilt-oriented cultures of the West. Politically forgiveness can only be seen as indulgence and becomes problematic.

In Jesus' indigenous culture, repentance could become the justifying ground for the king's forgiveness if he so chose. While it did not merit or deserve forgiveness, if forgiveness was granted, no further sacrificial penalty was required to adjust a moral imbalance. Sacrifices were not viewed as penalties. They were ritual acts symbolical of repentance.

Sacrifice represented the offender's recognition and acknowledgement of the moral enormity of sin and genuine *metanonia*, i.e., the sincere intent to change one's moral course. It is a *penitential offering* of sorrow and regret, and a pledge of reconciliation and transformation. It represents the conscious participation in and acceptance of God's forgiveness. Thus when we come to realize the enormity of humanity's crucifixion of Christ and genuinely repent, he becomes our *sacrifice* for sin, and potentially for the whole world. Interpreting his death as an autonomous moral act that balances the ledgers of heaven and justifies God in indulging the human race simply accommodates the mission of the Messiah to the old *lex talionis*.

Forgiveness and Restorative Justice

This does not imply, however, that forgiveness infers condoning, conniving with, or henceforth tolerating abusive or unjust action. Forgiveness restores the social relationship (hopefully also the personal) and clears the way to a fair adjustment of the offense *with the assumption that it will not continue*. Where restitution is impossible, as in the case of murder, forgiveness becomes an iconic symbol of empathy and restored social equilibrium that in itself recognizes the seriousness of the offense. It does not absolve the perpetrator of responsibility. It does not excuse the offense.

Jesus did not define juridical justice as retributive but rather as corrective or restorative of a status quo ante. Describing a Mennonite perspective on social justice, J. Lawrence Burkholder maintains that a "responsible society" is a society in which justice "is not conceived arbitrarily as the mechanical division of goods and privileges but as a concern for the total situation." Then he comments further, "[Social] justice is simply the ability to see one's self and one's interest in the total social context with a view to the general welfare."[36] Beginning with such a conception of the just society, corrective justice is that judgment which engenders a just peace. Thus a politics of repentance and forgiveness is offered as a realistic vindication of the right by rectifying or setting right the injustice and fractured relationships. It does not make punitive retaliatory demands but rather makes demands for reasonable reparations and corrective change that will prevent the continuation or repetition of the offense.[37]

In his *No Future Without Forgiveness*, Desmond Tutu describes how the Truth and Reconciliation Commission wrestled with this problem and concluded that the basic issue has to do with the definition of justice as retaliation. His observation is worth quoting.

> One might go on to say that perhaps justice fails to be done only if the concept we entertain of justice is retributive justice, whose chief goal is to be punitive, so that the wronged party is really the state, something impersonal, which has little consideration for the real victims and almost none for the perpetrator.
>
> We contend that there is another kind of justice, restorative justice, which was characteristic of traditional African jurisprudence. Here the central concern is not retribution or punishment. In the spirit of *ubuntu*, the central concern is the healing of breaches, the redressing of imbalances, the restoration of broken relationships, a seeking to rehabilitate both the victim and the perpetrator, who should be given the opportunity to be reintegrated into the community he has injured by his offense.[38]

We must insist that forgiveness, as a political act, does not cover continuing injustice and violence that can and should be rectified. In the justice process, forgiveness is organically related to repentance that alters the future. That is, repentance as a political act is more than being sorry for the past. It is metanonia, a change of orientation and behavior that includes willingness to compensate the victim for past violations in so far as possible. Here the example of Zacchaeus (Luke 19) comes to mind. If forgiveness is to be a means to restorative justice, it must be accompanied by repentance in the one forgiven. Where it is absent *aphiemi* (forgiveness) can only take the form of *letting go* anger and resentment both subjectively in personal reconciliation and in social "forgetting." In this case justice can only take the form not of retaliation but of protecting the public from the repetition of the offense.

Forgiveness is a way of dealing with offenses that defy human restoration, but this cannot satisfy the moral demands of justice without a genuine change for the future. Only God can wipe away, erase, forget the injustice, e.g., the violence of the past in which countless millions have been massacred in greed and vengeance. God's forgiveness, however, cannot be realized apart from our mutual repentance and forgiving of each other. God's forgiveness does not mean that a divine power indulges wrongdoing apart from our participation in forgiving. The only wisdom saying from Jesus that may have bearing on the outcome where repentance is not forthcoming is Matthew 5:25-26, "Come to terms quickly with your accuser while you are on the way to court . . . [or] you will never get out until you have paid the last penny." There is no hint in the sayings of Jesus that despite intransigent persistence in wrongdoing the moral consequences of our evil deeds will be erased!

Forgiveness as portrayed in the life and teachings of Jesus is to be understood as an alternate to vengeful, punitive retaliation as a way of ending conflict and violence. It is a way of ending the ongoing cycle of alienation and conflict by interpreting the *redress* of wrong as *rectification* rather than *requital* or retaliation. It does not define justice as an equation of violence suffered and violence done plus appropriate deterrent punishment. Rather it focuses on putting right the offending situation and transforming the offender. It focuses on the victim-offender relationship rather than a balance of the legal system.

Focusing on transformation, whether individual or social, rather than on punitive retaliation as the goal of justice is not to be confused with condoning or indulging wrongdoing. Not only do we not condone or indulge the wrong done, we also no longer tolerate it. Forgiving is a way of clearing the ground so reconstruction can take place. It is a way of letting go the festering memory of wrong done, a kind of intentional forgetting, as when God says he will no longer remember our sins. Forgiveness as it is demonstrated in the life, death, and resurrection of Christ erases the effects of the offensive action by transforming the dynamics of relationship. In this sense forgiveness is a dialectical necessity to achieving justice.

Jesus did not offer this as a utopian ideal. He offered it as a realistic alternative, and his disciples understood that they had been commissioned to disciple the nations, teaching them to follow his pattern. Thus when Israel rejected this calling, his disciples extended the call to include the Gentiles and universalized the movement.

Notes

1. *The Historical Jesus: The Life of a Mediterranean Jewish Peasant* (New York: Harper Collins, 1991), 423.

2. John Dominic Crossan and Jonathan L. Reed, *Excavating Jesus Beneath the Stones, Behind the Texts* (San Francisco: Harper, 2001). He compares the textual layers to the layers of artifacts found in archeological excavations. For a rigorous working out of this methodology one should see his *The Historical Jesus: The Life of a Mediterranean Peasant* (San Francisco: Harper Collins, 1991). In his epilogue to the book he wrote, "It [this book] presumes that there will always be divergent historical Jesuses, that there will alwayshe be divergent Christs built upon them, but, above all, it argues that the structure of a Christianity will always be: *this is how we see Jesus-then as Christ-now*. I am proposing that the dialectic between Jesuses and Christs . . . is at the heart of both tradition and canon, that it is perfectly valid, has always been with us and probably always will be," 423.

3. Perry Bush gives an excellent, brief descriptive characterization of the state of affairs in the twentieth century. Now that war has become "*total* war," he asks, "How does one retain conscientious scruples against war in a nation at total war? Pacifists would have to wrestle with this question with increasing vigor in the twentieth century." See *Two Kingdoms, Two Loyalties: Mennonite Pacifism in Modern America* (Baltimore: The Johns Hopkins University Press, 1998), 13-19.

4. See Adolph Harnack's *The Essence of Christianity* first published in 1900. Later liberal theology adopted the "social gospel."

5. James H. Charlesworth, *Jesus Within Judaism: New Light from Exciting Archaeological Discoveries* (New York: Doubleday, 1988), 16, italics added.

6. N. T. Wright, *The Challenge of Jesus: Rediscovering Who Jesus Was and Is* (Downers Grove. Ill.: InterVarsity Press, 1999), 58. "I therefore propose that the clash between

Jesus and his Jewish contemporaries, especially the Pharisees, must be seen in terms of alternative political agendas generated by alternative eschatological beliefs and expectations. Jesus was announcing the kingdom in a way that did not reinforce but rather called into question the agenda of revolutionary zeal that dominated the horizon of, especially, the leading group within Pharisaism." See especially chapter 2, "The Challenge of the Kingdom."

7. Already according to 1 Samuel 8:4-8, Israel's demand to have a king and a political identity "like other nations" was interpreted as a rejection of the kingship of Yahweh.

8. See Martin Hengel, *Judaism and Hellenism: Studies in their Encounter in Palestine during the Early Hellenistic Period* (Philadelphia: Fortress, 1974, 1981) on the development of the Jewish wisdom tradition, especially "Wisdom and Torah in Pharisaic and Rabbinic Judaism," vol. 1, 169-175.

9. Donald Shriver summarizes his message in three pithy phrases, "sharing of food and clothing, no cheating in business, 'no bullying, no blackmail' in soldiering." See *An Ethic for Enemies: Forgiveness in Politics* (New York: Oxford University Press, 1995), 37.

10. Ben Witherington III, *The Jesus Quest: The Third Search for the Jew of Nazareth* (Downers Grove: Intervarsity Press, 1997), 192. Witherington make the point that the classification of prophet or sage is not exclusive. One could be both. See also his *Jesus the Sage: The Pilgrimage of Wisdom* (Minneapolis: Augsburg Fortress), 1994.

11. Jesus' role as a teacher of wisdom—an alternative wisdom, but wisdom nonetheless—is widely recognized by contemporary Jesus scholars. See Marcus Borg, *Meeting Jesus Again for the First Time* (San Francisco: Harper Collins, 1995), especially chapters 4 and 5.

E. P. Sanders, in his *The Historical Figure of Jesus* (Allen Lane: The Penguin Press, 1993), emphasizes Jesus' regard for himself "as having full authority to speak and act on the behalf of God," and thus characterizes him as a "charismatic and autonomous prophet", in contrast to "a rabbi, or teacher of the law, [who] derived authority from studying and interpreting the Bible" (p. 238). Both Witherington and Borg, however, point to his designation as the "Wisdom/Word" of God as recognition of his immediate relationship to God. Indeed, Witherington agrees with Marinus de Jung who cites Luke 10:21-22/Matthew 11:25-27 as evidence that identifying Jesus as the Wisdom of God "may express the essence of Jesus' relationship to God in a way that goes beyond all the traditional titles," 188-189. I am inclined to agree with Witherington, although my immediate concern is with the hermeneutical significance of such a classification.

12. Marcus Borg, *Meeting Jesus Again for the First Time* (San Francisco: Harper Collins, 1995), 71.

13. *The Jesus Quest*, p. 187.

14. Archibald M. Hunter, *A Pattern for Life: An Exposition of the Sermon on the Mount* (Philadelphia: Westminster Press, 1953).

15. This is the title of yet another manual of instruction by John W. Miller. See *The Christian Way: A Guide to the Christian Life Based on the Sermon on the Mount* (Scottdale, Pa.: Herald Press, 1969).

16. Hans Conzelmann, *The Theology of St. Luke* (Philadelphia: Fortress Press, 1982), 26.

17. *Jesus Within Judaism*, 16.

18. "I take this obscure saying to be a warning on the part of Jesus against those who imagined that the Kingdom could be established by armed force and political revolution. To anyone who could read the signs of the times it was obvious that fanatical patriotism was a current that was steadily gaining strength and was destined to end in a flood of disasters. The saying that they who take the sword shall perish by the sword was only too abundantly fulfilled, first in A.D. 70 and again in the calamitous revolt in the reign of Hadrian"; T. W. Manson, *The Teaching of Jesus: Studies of its Form and Content* (Cambridge: University Press, 1935; 1963 paper ed.), 124, fn.

19. In his chapter, "Nonresistance, Nonviolent Resistance, and Power," written in the 1970s J. Lawrence Burkholder distinguished between "the [absolute] nonresistance of the cross and what led to the cross." He continues, "We must not draw from this, however, that the decision to be nonviolent was a decision to be nonresistant in the sense that there is no place in the service of God for resistance. . . *the issue is not between nonviolence and nonresistance, but between violence and various forms of nonviolence*" (italics his). See J. R. Burkholder and Calvin Redekop, editors, "*Kingdom Cross and Community*" (Scottdale, Pa.: Herald Press, 1976), 134-35.

This intuited moral distinction certainly provides an authentic perspective from which to read the Gospels. What to my knowledge has not been done in Mennonite circles is to examine the hermeneutical basis for such a distinction.

20. Earl Zimmerman notes that "The phrase 'biblical nonresistance' was commonly used by North American Mennonites to describe their position in the 1950s. The phrase was taken from Jesus' command not to resist an evildoer (Matt. 5:39). This description served to distinguish their position from liberal Protestant and Gandhian positions. The term "nonresistance" was also used more broadly by Christian scholars to describe Jesus' response to violence. See Jean Lasserre, *War and the Gospel* (London: James Clark & Co. Ltd, 1962), 35. The problem with the term was that it connoted a passivity that many Mennonites were not comfortable with. It shares that problem with the more common term 'pacifism,' which is used to define a principled opposition to war. In the following decades, Mennonites moved toward more engaged language such as 'peacebuilding' and 'active nonviolence'." See "A Praxis of Peace: The "Politics of Jesus" According to John Howard Yoder," unpublished dissertation (Catholic University of America, 2004), 77, fn.

Of course this passive interpretation of Jesus' teachings has not been the view only of Mennonites. Reinhold Niebuhr assumes its validity in his argument against the nonresistant position. Rabbi Jacob Neusner in his *A Rabbi Talks with Jesus*, quoted by Marlin Miller, understands Jesus the same way. "[T]he Torah knows nothing of non resisting evil and does not value either the craven person, who submits, or the arrogant person, who holds that it is beneath one's dignity to oppose evil. Passivity in the face of evil serves the purpose of evil. The Torah calls eternal Israel always to struggle for God's purpose; the Torah sanctions warfare and recognizes legitimate power. So I find amazing Jesus' statement that it is a religious duty to fold before evil." See Willard M. Swartley, ed., *Violence Renounced: Rene Girard, Biblical Studies, and Peacemaking* (Telford, Pa.: Pandora Press U.S., 2000), 36.

21. The superiority of their social ethic was widely recognized in the Roman world of Jesus' day, and many Gentiles were attracted to it even when they did not join the

group's self-image. One did not have to make a rational ethical case or philosophical analysis of the difference to justify exclusion. The danger was intuited. It was viewed as defiling and dangerous, and it could pollute the whole lump like spoiled leaven.[5]

The *justice codes*, on the other hand, have to do with personal, socioeconomic, and political relationships that define how society functions. They define the equitable and right behavior Yahweh expects. True, justice too is culturally conditioned, but at their best the codes call for integrity, honesty, empathy, and respect for the other person as "the image of God." In short they call for an intra-group ethic of loving one's neighbor as one's self, which includes the foreigners among them (19:18). Both purity taboos and ethical norms were handed down by God who commanded, "You shall be holy to me; for I the Lord am holy, and I have separated you from the other peoples to be mine" (20:26; 19:2).

By and large the taboos regulate physical purity and are closely related to ritual standards of purity for the priesthood.[6] They issue from sacred tradition and mystery—the will of Yahweh—and dereliction in their observance threatens danger, illness, and misfortune. While such proscriptions define cultural morality, they do not necessarily indicate non-ethical behavior.

On the other hand, the ethical commands, though defined in terms of local ancient norms and values, do speak to functional norms of social-personal justice—just relationships (Mic. 6:8). In the Torah they, like the cultic taboos, are simply presented as the word of the Lord through Moses, but they are obligatory because they promote fair, respectful, compassionate human intercourse. They have the character of universal human norms.

As we will observe in what follows, the prophetic base for biblical morality shifts over the sweep of Hebrew history from cultic to ethical, from traditional taboos to prophetic norms that emerge as the "word of the Lord" in the evolving cultural situation. We can trace a trajectory from obligation based on divine (mystical) ancestral tradition to experiential, goal oriented (teleological) social norms, from ceremony to character, from genetic/physical (relation to clan) to faith/spiritual (social-personal) relationships. The genius of the Bible is that it is a historical revelation, which can be and has been adapted to changing human cultural.

Getting to the Present

The difficulty of transferring these commands from their ancient setting to our Western culture—from cultic taboo to ethical norm—stems partly from the undifferentiated character of the codes and the overlapping of ethical and ritual categories. How, for example, are the various sexual regulations to be classified? Some of them, like the incest laws, stem from the ancient polygamous definitions of family relationships. Some stem from mistaken notions of blood pollution. Others derive from the assumed rights of males over females, the hierarchical stratification of the religio-social order, wrong notions about the male's role in conception, and the female menstrual cycle. The theological question here in contrast to the historical-critical question is not whether and when God commanded ancient Israel to abide by these regulations, but how to authentically contextualize them in our society.

Complicating still more the task of transcultural application of these holiness laws is the fact that the two categories cannot be entirely separated. Some cultic taboos such as keeping of the Sabbath as well as the proscription of idolatry and child sacrifice are clearly related to the social welfare of society (an ethical end). And incest laws regulating sexual activity protect women of the extended family from sexual abuse.

But this last example raises another kind of difficulty in making the transfer from ancient to contemporary culture. What is the definition of ethical justice in the ancient culture? Some of the Levitical concepts of ethical justice are culturally conditioned by concepts of personal and social relationships that are morally unacceptable today. What sexual behaviors, for example, are considered "abusive"? And what justifies their prohibition?

In the Levitical world, when a slave woman was raped, "justice" required that her master be properly compensated, not the woman! Indeed, adultery, considered an ethical infringement, was so evaluated not because the woman had been abused but because her owner-husband's social status had been damaged. If a son had sexual intercourse, whether rape or otherwise, with one of his father's wives, the father's honor must be vindicated by putting the wife as well as the son to death (20:11). And how shall we evaluate and apply the death penalty for cursing one's parents (20:9), which was evidently considered just and necessary?

We observe, then, that the morality of the Levitical holiness code is both cultic and ethical, emphasizing in turn both tribal purity and social-ethical relationships such as compassion and justice. The tribal purity taboos are defined as practices that distinguish the Israelites from the Egyptians and Canaanites (Lev. 18:1), which are an "abomination" to the Lord. This separation, or purity (the biblical word is "holiness") itself is the moral sanction that validates and enforces the taboos.

This, then, brings us to the nub of the question this chapter addresses. How shall we classify the restrictions against incest, bestiality, adultery, sex during menstruation, male same-sex sexual activity (Female same-sex behavior is not addressed)? And how shall we distinguish between the ethical and the cultic purity elements involved? How shall we recalibrate the moral features of incest as defined in a polygamous culture, and what makes it taboo? What are the grounds for maintaining that same-sex erotic behavior is despicable and repulsive to the God revealed to us in Jesus Christ while coitus during menstruation is not (20:18)?

Taboos and Revelation

The religious instruction recorded in the book of Leviticus is presented as the dictated communication of Yahweh through Moses. The book opens with these words, "The Lord summoned Moses and spoke to him from the tent of meeting, saying: *Speak to the people of Israel and say to them. . .*" (vv. 1-2). This immediately raises the hermeneutical question of its cross-cultural translation and application. How do such unambiguous *instructions to ancient Israel,* setting it apart from the surrounding nations, transfer across the centuries and cultures of humankind? Obviously in this case many of the cultic practices have been dropped or superceded even by Israel. But many conservative Christians and Jews still insist that the sexual taboos, at least some of them, are the enduring and transcultural word of the Lord. How shall we understand and apply these religious taboos of an ancient society that claim the authority of God for the regulation of human society?[7]

One should note the slight but significant difference in describing the problem as "cross-cultural" or "transcultural." The transcultural approach to the problem of contextualization begins with the assumption that revelation contains both supra-cultural commands that are universally and eternally valid and commands that are "culture-based" and thus "culturally confined." Only the latter are limited to the time and place of their issue.[8] Thus in the words of Darrell Bock, who writes the forward for Terrance Tiessen's *Slaves, Women and Homosexuals*, one must approach the texts both "biblically and culturally" (p. 9).

The cross-cultural perspective asks how the culturally conditioned revelation to Israel is properly applied to other cultures, whether in geographical space or temporal history. The cross-cultural approach assumes that all revelation is historically, i.e., culturally, conditioned. This includes "biblical" revelation, which in fact was modified as Israel's historical situation changed. Thus assuming the relevance of scriptural revelation, it asks the question how a revelation received by ancient Israel as authoritative can be authentically transferred to other cultures.

There is no clear line of distinction between culturally evolved notions and religiously disclosed beliefs and practices for anthropologists to appeal to. Theologically stated, this means that no distinct hermeneutical line can be drawn between divine revelation and its cultural perception and response. Revelation inevitably is transmitted through the medium of a particular cultural ideology, and a religious taboo claiming its source as revelation is the expression of a particular culture. Religious belief and practice is one aspect of culture irrespective of its claim to have its source in revelation. Thus to speak as precisely as possible, the Mosaic Torah is *Israel's culturally conditioned witness and response* to God's self-disclosure to the ancient Hebrews.

To recognize that its reception is culturally conditioned does not in itself discount its status as revelation, but it does clearly affect the hermeneutical process by which a religious taboo is applied to other cultures. All revelation has come in a temporal and spatial human context and is conditioned by its limited and fallible receptors. One cannot, therefore, assume that because it is recognized as revelation to ancient Israel it is universally applicable without adaptation. Because revelation is given in a particular cultural context, its cross-cultural transmission must take into account the differences that exist across human cultures. We refer to this process as contextualization, and this applies to all revelation.

The legislation of the sexual codes in Leviticus 18–22, as we have seen, has the generic status of a taboo or "ritual prohibition." A taboo is considered a protective measure against harm from the mysterious supernatural power. It is a cultural prohibition based on a supernatural command, and it is its supernatural origin that gives it moral authority.

Fear and/or reverence of its supernatural source enforce the taboo. As we noted above, this does not imply that the Levitical taboos are not revelation. Indeed, it would seem to underscore their "revealed" character. But strictly speaking it does highlight their nature as covenantal proscriptions, and characterizes their moral status as social custom rather than ethical rationale. Shame and fear generally enforce such protective social customs.

The social and moral legislation of Leviticus 18–20 fits this description precisely. The proscriptions are presented as the direct verbal commandments of the Lord to Moses, and they are based on the relation of national Israel to Yahweh alone. For example, male same-sex acts are "an abomination" to Yahweh, and when a male owner has sexual relations with a female slave, he shall "bring a guilt offering to Yahweh" (19:21). If social or physical consequences of these actions are assumed, they are not made the moral reason for the prohibition.

To identify the revelation in Leviticus, then, as having to do with taboos implies its human, cultural limitation and relativity. The code applies immediately and directly to ancient Israelite society in its historical situation. It is God's revelation to and for Israel as God's special people. Yahweh's identity is bound together with Israel's identity. Yahweh is Israel's God, and Israel is Yahweh's people. That is their essential cultural self-identity. "Israel is the Lord's own portion" (Sirach 17:17). Yahweh is conceived as Israel's authoritative archetype, and collectively Israel is to be the human representation of Yahweh. Conversely God's will is identified with, i.e., virtually equivalent to, Israel's cultural self-image.

Yahweh's nation does not describe its self-identity in theological or philosophical terms but in moral commandments and group practices that mark it as Yahweh's own nation. Holiness is conceptualized as a consecration, a setting apart, of Israel as Yahweh's people, and holiness is defined in an ethnic cultural pattern that distinguishes Israel from the nations around them. How then does this holiness ethic become a universal moral demand?

Briefly put, the universalization of this ethnic, tribal holiness code is arrived at theologically. Its universality rests on the supremacy of Yahweh over all other gods. Since Yahweh is the one and only recognized deity, by implication the moral obligation for Hebrew society applies to all nations. However, although Israel conceived the Lord to be universal in power and authority, Israel itself did not give the taboos universal application in its intercourse with the nations round about. And as we shall see Israel's conception of the moral character and will of God moves steadily in a trajectory from cultic to ethical holiness. Therefore, we cannot simply universalize either the requirements of Israel's religious practice or the prohibitions of its cultic taboos. Even though their source is recognized as *revelation* for Israel, the Levitical taboos cannot be simply identified as God's will for all the nations.

Moving from Old to New Testament

For those of us who have adopted this people of God identity through our recognition of Jesus as the messianic fulfillment of the first covenant and mediator of a new one, the identity of God as the Hebraic Yahweh must be taken seriously. Clearly God's universal authority as disclosed in Jesus is established in the new covenant. But our understanding of God mediated through Jesus Christ has necessitated the recalibration of our concepts of God's authority and its appropriation in society. Jesus has been absorbed as it were into the unity of the universal deity, and he rather than Hebrew culture has become the medium through which God's universal will is known.

This development in the monotheistic conception of God, which Larry Hurtado labels "binitarian,"[9] is further modified by the introduction of the Holy Spirit (of Jesus) into the trinitarian model of the one universal Deity. Such a development certainly indicates a methodological as well as an ontological change in ascertaining and appropriating the universal will of God in a global pluralism of cultures. Attempts at historical literalism and restitution are transcended by an authentic contextualization of the historical text in the Spirit of Jesus.

Do the taboos of the ancient Hebrews under the old covenant, even when recognized as Yahweh's will for that society, translate as universal ethical codes under the new covenant? Clearly many of them do not. The Levitical codes spell out the social patterns that distinguish God's special people from the nations around them. And even when we adopt the people of God identity and recognize God's supreme and universal in authority, we no longer define that universality in hierarchical terms of power with Israel as the defining cultural model. No longer is that authority administered as a uniform code from a Hebrew tabernacle or a hillside in Galilee.

It follows that a straight-line hermeneutic cannot be applied when defining and appropriating the holiness taboos of the Old covenant to the New. It is not merely a question of whether a given command in the Old is to be carried over to the New. The New Covenant offers a different kind of ethical evaluation of the taboos—not literal but ethical, one that requires taking into account the social, moral, and scientific understanding of the particular culture to which it is applied. The process of interpreting and transmitting Old Covenant proscriptions to New Covenant directives requires a transformation of the taboo into ethical admonition and principle that makes loving respect for others as creatures in the image of God paramount. Surely this is clearly implied in Jesus' words, "The Sabbath was made for humankind, and not humankind for the Sabbath" (Mark 2:27; Matt. 12: 1-12).

Neither can we argue that apostolic interpretations and applications of the taboos in the first-century Middle East culture, i.e., New Testament, are immutable. The apostolic canon is the inspired attempt to contextualize the Hebrew Scriptures and demonstrate their rapport with the gospel proclamation of Jesus as Messiah in the first century Gentile world. This required many reinterpretations and pragmatic adaptations in what were considered moral codes in Hebrew society. For example, witness the long debate over circumcision, eating of unclean food, and definition of sexual behaviors (incest and fornication), the God-ordained place of women, slavery, and the like.

Further, the transmission of the original teaching and example of Jesus to the Hellenistic world required considerable contextualization. In this process they were obliged to sort out which traditional rabbinic interpretations of the Old Testament fit into the new message about Jesus. Paul, for example, strenuously repudiated some rabbinic interpretations of the Torah, which he referred to as the "traditions of my ancestors" in Galatians 1:13-17. He rejected circumcision as the condition for receiving "Gentile sinners" into the church but retained other traditional Jewish social mores, such as a attitudes and customs associated with male headship—a father's autocratic authority and control over his daughters and women's subservience to men, which we today see as moral issues. And it seems clear to me that Paul, a "Hebrew of the Hebrews," also accepted without question the rabbinic prohibition of same-sex sexual practice as given in Leviticus for his first-century culture. He offers a theological justification for this position in much the same rabbinic pattern he employs to justify male headship in 1 Corinthians 11.

What Is at Issue

I am not attempting to argue that all of these issues are identical. Rather, my point is that taboos and morally binding customs, understood in their original cultural setting to be the dictated will of God, were open to adjustment in light of new knowledge and changing circumstances. Under the aegis of the Spirit of Christ, these were the first steps in a long progression of contextual paraphrases and applications of the message in the ongoing historical and geographical changes of cultures.

These steps also raise the fundamental question of finding an ethical rationale for theocratic taboos of an earlier time. Surely Jesus' own radical challenge of the cultic Sabbath regulation, which was the self-defining symbol of Hebrew identity, and his rejection of the social taboos that regulated the moral and religious life of the Jewish community offer precedent for this process.[10]

The changes of worldview in our Western culture from those of ancient traditional cultures—changes in scientific perspective, moral values, and sociopolitical relationships—have been especially radical and far-reaching. And, we might add, not all of these changes are deleterious or out of sync with New Testament values. It is precisely in our world, therefore, that contextualization must involve cultural re-evaluation as well as translation. That task involves evaluation of the ethical reasons behind the Hebrew proscriptions found in both covenants, and the validity of those reasons for the governance of any other given culture throughout the history of the world.

In both the Old and New Testaments, same-sex genital activity is clearly taboo. As such it is considered *sin*, i.e., disobedience of God's law. It is also a *legal* proscription in the Old and has the seriousness of a *moral* prohibition, not just an ethnic folkway. Taking this *religious* taboo seriously our question remains. What is the *ethical* warrant for the prohibition of erotic homosexual sexual behavior? In light of the shift in the ethical argument, as we shall see below, the question is whether and in what sense same-sex erotic sexual behavior is a *moral—hence sinful—perversion*, as we understand that term today.

As we have noted, the apostle Paul accepted without question the cultural categories of the traditional Hebrew religious taboo on homosexual activity and applied it to the churches of the Roman Empire. *The question for Christian ethics remains whether Paul's rabbinic theological rationale (compare 1 Cor. 11: 1-16) and cultural application establishes the Hebrew cultic regulation as God's universal moral command and ends the contextualization process.* I assume that it does not, although Paul's insight into his own cultural context must be carefully weighed.

Post-Traditional Christian Ethics

A fundamental shift in ethical syntax, a shift already presaged in the Hebrew prophets and then even more clearly in Jesus and the New Testament writings, has taken place in the Western Christian world. The shift has to do with the way in which religious, or cultic, taboos are related to the making of ethical judgments, and it has taken several thousand years to sort itself out. Greek rationalism was undoubtedly the midwife assisting its birth in Western society, but it is not the child merely of Stoic reason. As Joseph Kotva notes in his *The Christian Case for Virtue Ethics,*

> It is now almost impossible to view moral rules as purely objective and unchanging. Indeed, we can show that many norms and rules reflect development and the influence of the historical contexts in which they were formulated. Thus, for example, Catholic rules governing contraception and Mennonite norms concerning head coverings have undergone considerable change.[11]

Traditionally in sacral societies both moral and legal rules have been based on authoritative religious premises. Contemporary Western societies have substituted an anthropological premise for a religious one. Personal and social well-being provide the basis for the definition, evaluation, and sanction of moral action. Nor is this merely the result of secularization. It is at least in part a continuation of an ethical trajectory in the Hebrew prophets and the New Testament that we will note below.

Christian theological ethics has recognized this and has adjusted its theological rationale accordingly. It has maintained its religious base by equating human welfare with the will of God. The theological rationale for this adjustment is the biblical teaching that humans are created *in*

God's image, and that God is *Abba*—"the Father from whom every family in heaven and on earth takes its name" (Eph. 3:14). This pattern of reasoning is true across the Protestant theological spectrum, even in conservative evangelical circles. For example, while organizations like Focus on the Family accept the Hebrew taboos as revelation, they base their *moral* argument against legalizing same-sex unions on its threat to the stability of the nuclear heterosexual family, which they hold to be God's original will for the welfare of human society.

Even though the phrase *under God* has been retained in the self-definition of U.S. national identity, we make overlapping distinctions between the religious and the moral. Religious virtue we call *piety*, and trespass of religious statutes we classify as *sin*. We make the *cultic* a distinct category distinguishing it from the *legal* and *moral*, and we distinguish between cultic taboo (religious), political legislation (legal), and ethical requirement (social).

With biblical sanction, we identify God's holiness as ethical/moral virtue rather than cultic separation. God's moral holiness is understood as God's character displayed in justice, compassion, and patience. The moral vision for human individuals and society is likewise the achievement of a life-affirming *character*, which expresses itself in maximizing the mutual good. I would argue that it is this more nuanced kind of ethical analysis and not simply exegetical interpretation and literal application of the biblical text that must provide the basis for our moral discernment.

In his *Homosexuality: Biblical Interpretation and Moral Discernment*, Willard Swartley makes much of the hermeneutical difference between the scriptural treatment of subjects like Sabbath, war, the role of women, and slavery on the one hand—and same-sex genital practice on the other. Of the former subjects, he writes,

> From a *surface* [sic] analysis one observes mixed signals in the biblical texts on slavery and the role of women. . . Conversely, all the texts that speak of same-sex practice are of the same mind. In explicit Scripture statements, homosexual practice, i.e., same-sex genital intercourse, is always wrong.[12]

If by "surface analysis" Swartley means literal reading of the text in its ancient setting and language, this observation can hardly be challenged. But it is not Swartley's exegesis that is being questioned on this point.

Rather, it is the hermeneutical adequacy of such exegesis without a theological hermeneutic that recognizes the moral trajectory in biblical and church history that is being called into question.

There is clearly a more profound biblical trajectory defining the holiness required by God that must be taken into account. It moves from legal and cultic prescriptions of holiness to holiness as a relationship and attitude of the heart; from holiness defined as tabooed religious practices or required cultic rituals to holiness as virtuous ethical and spiritual character. It progresses from holiness as sacred time, space, and objects to holy people who make up the "living stones" of God's temple (1 Pet. 2: 4-5). This trajectory is evident in the movement from Israel's theological-cultural identity based on outward Hebrew ethnicity to identity based on inward character and voluntary relationship to Israel's God (Rom. 2:28-29).

We can trace this trajectory, which reaches a definitive point in Christ, on many levels in the evolving religious and moral milieu of Israel. In the sphere of religious identity it moves from "circumcision of the flesh" to "circumcision of the heart." In worship from cultic ritual to worship "in spirit and in truth" (John 4:23-24). In morals from external purity codes to "Blessed are the pure in heart" (Matt. 5: 8). In societal regulations from the law written on stone to law written on the heart (Jer. 31: 31-34). In family relationships from patriarchal marriage structures where divorce is a matter of legal definition to mutual dependence, respect, and affection. "Nonconformity to this world," which is Paul's description of holiness, means transformation and renewing of the mind so that genuine love, inspiring hope, and commitment to the cause of Christ become the focus of life (Rom. 12:1-21). This trajectory is of essential importance as a hermeneutical perspective in applying sexual taboos across cultures.

One must ask, therefore, what is the *ethical* warrant apart from religious or cultic regulations for making judgments about all sexual relationships? This has become a major issue for evangelical churches during the last half century in defining the religious parameters permitted in heterosexual relationships. What qualifies as *moral* or *immoral* in sexual relationships? And if judged to be moral, ought not such relationships be religiously permissible? Over the past century, the evangelical churches have changed many heterosexual taboos which were considered moral infringements in their pastoral disciplines.[13] If the church in modification of its past disciplines discerns that a private sexual activity is moral despite earlier religious taboos (biblical or otherwise), may it not henceforth permit such behavior as at least religiously indifferent?

As an obvious example of this process, we can site the changed religious attitudes and practice involving menstruating women (Lev. 20:18). The church no longer considers this and other until recently abhorred heterosexual "joys of sex" to be taboo so long as abuse is not involved, and therefore no longer makes a *religious* issue of them. In a similar way, the taboo against masturbation, which in Protestant as well as Catholic circles was considered a highly immoral act by past generations, has been re-evaluated. *The same moral and spiritual discernment that has led to the modification of rules for heterosexual lifestyles should be applied to the moral evaluation of gay and lesbian lifestyles.* It is not enough to establish that same-sex lifestyles were strictly taboo on religious grounds in ancient biblical cultures.

The hermeneutical trajectory, which we have observed, implies a shift in the ethical argument that is crucial for understanding the differences in approach between the gay hermeneutic and the traditional evangelical hermeneutical perspective. Based on a paradigm already implicit in its definition of revelation, the evangelical tradition argues that the warrant for the proscription of same-sex sexual intimacy is the revealed will of God. Thus the taboo is presented as a moral absolute and an essential transcultural obligation—the classical *deontological* approach to ethical instruction. The ethical warrant for the proscription (taboo) or prescription is simply the perceived will of the ruler, which in this case is God. The obligatory force of the regulation rests on the hierarchically defined divine legislation. Gay hermeneutics, on the other hand, tend to use a *teleological* approach, which evaluates the ethical character of behavior by its outcome or *telos*.

In her chapter, "Theological Reflections on Aspects of Modern Medical Science," Mary Seller, an Anglican priest and professor of development genetics, argues for the practice of *in vitro* fertilization even though it involves the risk of some fertilized eggs being destroyed. She frames her argument in terms of God's intention for creatures made "in God's image," recognizing that the image is a developing reality, "not simply a one-off event." Then at the close of her chapter she notes that her argument has been "*consequentialist*," a form of the teleological approach, and not deontological. She explains that "deontological theory is governed by absolute imperatives and inherent rules for living," while teleological theory constantly tests moral legitimacy by an appeal to the probable and wanted ends in view.[14]

As I read this it occurred to me that this methodological difference is clearly represented on the one hand in the approaches of lesbian and gay theologians, and on the other in the more traditional evangelical approaches. Lesbian and gay perspectives tend to argue from consequences—a teleological approach—rather than traditional authority. They justify erotic desire and behavior by its *ends* (love), and not by a physical complementarity of male and female bodies for procreative purposes (sex). It might be argued that both of these approaches are consistent with different aspects of the biblical message, and a clear, consistent hermeneutical methodology needs to be agreed upon. The continuing dialogue needs to address and evaluate this fundamental difference in perspective.

I would argue that Paul's approach represents a fundamental change in understanding the nature and sanction for moral behavior which pushes us toward a more experiential approach. The shift is from ethnic religious taboos defining a particular religious culture to an ethical standard that is potentially applicable universally. In religious terms it is a shift from sacred tradition to direction by the Spirit of Jesus. The significance of this change for hermeneutics is enormous.

If we evaluate the question whether same-sex sexual relations are in themselves a moral perversion, according to a literal reading of biblical taboos the answer is yes. But we are not bound by the literal taboos. Thus we must ask the contextual question, namely, What have we learned and what cultural changes have occurred that might affect our understanding and application of this taboo? Discernment in contemporary global cultures may lead the church to a variety of positions on this or any other behavioral issues. To direct our process the church has the Holy Spirit and the precedent of Jesus and the apostolic church as a guide.

In Conclusion: Finding Right Questions

In closing let me state explicitly what I hope has become obvious in the above analysis—namely, that the theological and hermeneutical issues raised in the debate on human sexuality go far beyond the definition of the nature and role of sex. For Christians who take the authority of the Bible seriously, the issues include questions about the nature of biblical revelation, its interpretation, and its contextualization in radically different cultures. To get at this question we need more than scholarly academic exegesis of the biblical text within a traditional hermeneutical perspective. And we need a more nuanced and evenhanded analysis (exegesis) of the contemporary cultural situation that is not restricted to an exegetically deduced prototype of Saint Paul's description of first-century paganism.[15]

I have not argued that there are no ethical and moral ramifications to be considered in the discussion of same-sex relationships or that biblical perspectives on the subject are passé. Rather, I have attempted to clarify the nature of the issues that must be considered in the hermeneutical process of contextualization. In the discussion of sexuality, ethical and philological categories have been hopelessly confused in previous generations, and unfortunately they continue to be frustratingly ambiguous in much of the discussion today. We in the church obviously need to clarify our terminology and arrive at some agreement on methodology if we are to actually talk with rather than past each other.

The debate about same-sex erotic behavior has in fact raised fundamental questions about the nature and role of human sexuality. Or perhaps we should say that it has pushed many questions already implicit in the debate about heterosexual sexual practice to their logical conclusion. In our materialistic and hedonistic Western culture, the non-Christian, in fact, unchristian, gay/queer movement has pressed the implications of the sexual revolution to their logical secular extreme, but one should not identify the Christian gay/queer movement with its secular and pagan counterparts!

From the perspective of the traditional Roman Catholic theological rationale, which still forms the subconscious basis of evangelical Protestant positions, to speak of a Christian gay or lesbian theological perspective seems oxymoronic. But, to be candid, evangelical Protestantism has so thoroughly eviscerated the traditional position on heterosexual sexual practice in general that it has trouble expounding a consistent, biblically based position on homosexuality. In this situation, our Christian lesbian and gay sisters and brothers are challenging us to consider a non-traditional theological ethical perspective that is faithful to the intrinsic message of the gospel and the transformation of moral character after the pattern of Christ.

Notes

1. In his Frazer Lecture, "*Taboo,*" given at Cambridge in 1939 A. R. Radcliffe-Brown argued for the use of the term "ritual prohibition" rather than taboo. By ritual, however, he does not mean to limit the term to ceremonial prohibitions. Taboos are social prescriptions that have a magical or religious rather than secular (profane) rational basis. Their purpose is to define and facilitate "the social fabric in all the various sides or elements of it which we describe as religious, social, political, moral, and economic." *Reader in Comparative Religion: An Anthropological Approach*, Lessa William and Evon Vogt, editors (New York: Harper & Row, 1965), 112-123.

2. David Freedman writes, "The so-called Holiness Code (Lev. 17-26) is a summary catchall of legal prescriptions, cultic regulations, and moral exhortation, which may well have served as a catechism for some sanctuary school, or as a guide for priests and levites in their work as teachers of the people." (*The Interpreter's Dictionary of the Bible*, Volume 3, Nashville: Abingdon Press), 722.

3. John Dominic Crossan and Jonathan L. Reed, *Excavating Jesus: Beneath the Stones, Behind the Texts* (San Francisco: Harper, 2001), 171.

4. Walter Brueggemann speaks of the "tilt of holiness toward justice" observed in Leviticus itself, and doubts "the significance of these particular prohibitions [on homosexual relations] in the wider interpretive conversation on two counts." First, the holiness system is concerned with every facet of life, and "it is doubtful if these two particular verses of prohibition can be taken out of context when it is generally acknowledged that the wider holiness 'system' advocated here is not pertinent to contemporary Christian faith." Second, he says, "In theological interpretation it is not clear how a particular prohibition mentioned nowhere else in the commandments of Sinai is to be related to the wider sweep of the gospel. . . ." *An Introduction to the Old Testament: The Canon and Christian Imagination* (Louisville: Westminster John Knox Press, 2003), 71-73.

5. This is the difference between the proscriptions of Leviticus and the ethical writings of men like Plato and Aristotle who analyze and rationalize social structures and the morals that facilitate political order.

6. Mary Douglas makes a persuasive case for the cultic character of these taboos in *Leviticus as Literature* (New York: Oxford University Press, 1999), 236-238. She concludes that "the context is inescapably cultic. The perorations refer to defilement of the land, a grave situation which results from idolatry." See also her article, "Justice as the Cornerstone: An Interpretation of Leviticus 18-20" in *Interpretation*, 53 (October 1999), 341-350.

7. William J. Webb offers a carefully calibrated methodology for determining which scriptural commandments are "culture bound" and which are "transcultural. His method is premised on the assumption that all scripture while culturally affected, is still a verbally inerrant communication that includes both kinds of directives, and that by careful semantic and historical reading one can determine which directives are being adapted and which are not. Thus he concludes that "The homosexuality laws [in contrast to the laws on semen emission] are not part of ceremonial law, as can be seen from its severe penalty and the New Testament handling of homosexuality, in contrast to its treatment of ceremonial law," 170. *Slaves, Women and Homosexuals: Exploring the*

Hermeneutics of Cultural Analysis (Downers Grove: InterVarsity Press, 2001)

8. Ibid, 171.

9. *Lord Jesus Christ: Devotion to Jesus in Earliest Christianity* (Grand Rapids: Eerdmans, 2003), 51-53.

10. Crossan shows how radical Jesus' own rejection of current cultural religious norms was. "Since, moreover, Jesus lived out his own parable [The Great Banquet], the almost predictable counteraccusation to such open commensality [eating with sinners] would be immediate: Jesus is a glutton, a drunkard, and a friend of tax collectors and sinners. He makes, in other words, no appropriate distinctions and discriminations. And since women were present, especially unmarried women, the accusation would be that Jesus eats with whores, the standard epithet of denigration for any female outside appropriate male control." *Jesus: A Revolutionary Biography* (New York: Harper Collins, 1994), 69. This, of course, cannot be used in a direct way to argue that Jesus accepted those who flaunted the taboo on same-sex sexual practice, but it does indicate that he was open to the reinterpretation of cultic sexual taboos.

11. He continues, "The more aware we become of the fluid and changing nature of history, the more our moral judgments must attend to the details of the concrete situation. If nature and society are basically unchanging, then general principles are fine and we simply do whatever those before us did. But if nature and society change and develop, then we must attend to contextual variety and situational specificity." (Washington, D.C.: Georgetown University Press, 1996), 8-9)

12. Willard Swartley, *Homosexuality: Biblical Interpretation and Moral Discernment* (Scottdale, Pa.: Herald Press, c. 2003), 17.

13. See the carefully documented work of Peter Gardelia in his *Innocent Ecstasy: How Christianity Gave America an Ethic of Sexual Pleasure* (New York: Oxford University Press, 1985).

14. See *Growing into God,* 208-209, ed. Jean Mayland and published by Churches Together in Britain and Ireland as Lenten background material for 2004. It is available through CTBI Publications, 31 Great Smith Street, London SW1P 3BN.

15. This in a word seems to me to be the problem with Swartley's chapter 5, "Analysis of Contemporary Western Culture," in his *Homosexuality.*

7

An Anabaptist Spirituality for the Twenty-First Century

This chapter is a theological reflection on the significance of the original Anabaptist contextualization of Scripture and its use in the sixteenth-century world. I do not intend to revisit the debate about the sixteenth-century Anabaptist vision. Neither am I urging a "recovery" of a unified vision, implying that it has been lost or perverted and must be rediscovered and restored.[1] However, despite the focus on social history and the now widely accepted "polygenesis" theory of Anabaptist origins which have challenged the concept of a unified vision, no one doubts that there was a definable movement with characteristics that distinguish it from the magisterial movements of Luther, Zwingli, and Calvin. My concern is to explore the relevance of Anabaptism's unique perspectives as Mennonite and Brethren denominations that spring from that tradition look forward to life now—an era often labeled "postmodern."

By using the term *spirituality* I do not intend to raise the old question of spiritualists versus biblicists in the original movement. While there were those among the Anabaptists who relied on extra-scriptural revelations, such a subjectivist stance does not characterize the movement as a larger, continuing whole. And although the questions of literalism, legalism, and subjectivism are still relevant, perhaps, as John Oyer already implied in 1964, the issue is not between Bible and Spirit but comes down to the substitution of "Spirit" for "tradition" as the ultimate scriptural hermeneutic.[2] In contemporary terminology, A*nabaptists were free to contextualize the meaning of Scripture under the guidance of the Spirit of Christ as the spirit of the church.* In these terms, the issue is still extremely relevant for us today.

I have chosen the word *spirituality* partly because of its ambiguity. It suggests more than theology, ethics, hermeneutics, or ecclesiology. It also suggests more than the mere practice of religion, or piety. It locates the essence of the moral and social life in the lived experience of transcendence, which gives quality and character to our lives.

We may speak of spirituality as a kind of ethos, attitude, perspective, or style that characterizes our life in society. It encompasses our basic assumptions and definitions, our motivation, our conception of the mission, or purpose and goals, that define our responses and decisions. Thus we want to ask whether and how the lived experience of the Anabaptists in their quest to be faithful to their Christian calling might be relevant for our twenty-first century.

Recent Attempts at Defining Anabaptism

According to Werner Packull, Anabaptism represents a reform from below without government authorization, an empowerment of the common people, an emphasis on congregational authority aimed at communal salvation, and a practical reading of the gospel as a rule of life. Anabaptist theology, he notes, "was not the product of academic, professional theologians, but grew out of the collective experience of a community seeking to live out Christ's teaching."[3]

In his *Anabaptism and Asceticism,* Kenneth Davis proposes that Anabaptism was characterized by a monastic spirituality. The Anabaptists' deepest concern, he says, was for a new life of holiness that called for separation from the world, i.e., the ascetic principle. Arnold Snyder, in *The Life and Thought of Michael Sattler*, holds that a christocentric spirituality dominates the Anabaptist search for a practical ethical pattern. John Driver is convinced that "nonresistant suffering is fundamental" to understanding the Anabaptist vision of social justice. Thus he suggests a spirituality of messianic community in which the form of social concern is servanthood.[4]

John Oyer uses Harold S. Bender's terminology and speaks of "discipleship" as the overarching ethos. However, he elaborates the concept somewhat differently. For him a disciple's spirituality meant "separation from the world [of evil]," "a community life in which the sharing of material goods was the accepted practice," "suffering" and martyrdom, and "nonresistance," namely, "the repudiation of Christian participation in warfare."[5]

Locating this understanding of spirituality in the broader context of the other spiritual patterns of the Reformation will help us to see the significance of these characterizations. Lutheran spirituality, for example, may be characterized as a spirituality of grace with emphasis on the dynamic of the Word of God. Zwinglian spirituality was one of reform based on a humanistic hermeneutic of Scripture, while Calvin's was a spirituality of order based upon a theological hermeneutic of Scripture. By contrast Thomas Muentzer's was a spirituality of revolution based on a biblical ideal of social justice. Meanwhile the spirituality of the Anabaptists, those who survived and established an ongoing tradition, was a spirituality of obedient faith based on a christocentric understanding of Scripture. I am convinced that this is the heart of generic Anabaptism, and I will elaborate its characteristics that seem important for the way ahead.

Before doing so, however, I want to comment on the contextual intent of Harold Bender's original "Anabaptist Vision." Bender was operating in the context of an aging tradition, which was feeling the strains of cultural accommodation. The protagonist was a nondenominational Fundamentalism with strong nationalistic sympathies. He hoped to form Mennonitism into a viable institutional denomination held together by an authentic Anabaptist vision from the past and its institutional boards formed during the previous half century. Up until the 1980s, Mennonites could still say that these were the epoxy holding the denomination together. At present both have lost considerable potency. The denominational form is under the attack of a virulent individualism, and the vision is disintegrating under the relativism and egocentrism of postmodern pluralism.

It seems unlikely that we can put the denominational Humpty Dumpty together again in its old form. There is no doubt that the shell is seriously cracked, and the question remains whether there is a vision true to the original Anabaptist understanding of faith that can become the organizing focus for a new form in the twenty-first century. It is to be hoped that worldwide Mennonitism can find and contextualize such a generic essence that will provide a cultural identity for its diverse membership.

Characteristics of Anabaptist Spirituality

Anabaptism as a historically conditioned sixteenth-century response cannot serve as the comprehensive template for the future. One may hope, however, that we can be guided by more than the "evidences of imperfections, improvisations, and failings by the founding fathers [sic] of our tradition . . . as we grope to meet the challenges of our day," as Werner Packull suggests.[6] I want to suggest several characteristics pertinent to a useful contemporary contextualization. I have considered both the shape and needs of the present situation as well as the past in deciding which ones of highlight.

I propose the following five distinguishing characteristics of the sixteenth-century movement for our consideration: (1) a christocentric spirituality, (2) a spirituality of obedience, (3) a spirituality of the first beatitude, (4) a spirituality of nonviolent confrontation, and (5) a *Gemeinde* spirituality.

Christocentric Spirituality

Of course many traditions might quite properly claim to be christocentric. Therefore we must first give more specificity to the concept of Anabaptist christocentricity. In Anabaptism, Christ was not the focal point for mystic adoration, either in the earlier monastic or the later pietist sense. Further, he was not primarily the ontological center for a theology of incarnation. While Anabaptists were generally trinitarian in doctrine, they did not emphasize a theological definition of Christ as the second person of the Trinity.[7] Neither did their spirituality focus on him as a sacramental symbol for reverence. For them the culmination of worship was not a sacramental miracle performed by the church—but participation in the church as the sacramental body of Christ.

For them the goal of spirituality was the formation of the Christ image by the Holy Spirit through their faithful obedience. They understood *im Nachfolge den Weg Christi* as a spiritual formation in which, to use the words of Paul in Philippians 3:8-10, they came to know the deep meaning of Christ's suffering and thus found "a righteousness that comes through faith in Christ." In the words of Hubmaier, "The true and simple will of God is that we hold His beloved Son Christ Jesus before our eyes and follow his life and teaching. . . ."[8] This is impossible without grace. And as Kenneth Davis points out, "it relates to penitential exercises and their sanctifying powers."[9]

Nachfolge, or discipleship, was an internship in *Gelassenheit*, that is, yielding to the disciplining and enabling hand of God.[10] *Gelassenheit* does not indicate either passivity or self-depreciation. It means, rather, what the New Testament calls "meekness," or what Walter Wink in his *Engaging The Powers* describes as "nonviolence." Anabaptist discipleship was an apprenticeship in nonviolence and reconciliation under the guidance of the Master.

Although we cannot argue that there was a single focused vision, certainly there was a definitive christocentric center, much as there was a nonviolent core to the civil rights movement of the 1960s. Just as Anabaptists' biblicism was tempered by a christocentric focus, so was their spiritualism. Where their militancy turned to violence it was messianic. Where their message, as in the case of Hans Hut, was a gospel of creation, it was the cosmic Christ that was featured. The Holy Spirit of God, which moved in the world, was recognized as the Spirit of the Christ whom they met in their New Testament.

Their christocentric focus impacted their attitude toward the Bible. True, there are prominent examples of extreme biblical literalism. But at the other end of the spectrum were those who stressed the "inner word" and the immanent Christ. Underneath the literalistic tendencies the principle of a christocentric hermeneutic modified the literalism of men like Hubmaier, Denk, Marpeck, and Menno Simons.

Amid a contemporary worldwide revival of fundamentalist literalism, we need to stress this christocentric hermeneutic—not only as a grid for Old and New Testament interpretation but also for understanding and contextualizing individual passages in the New Testament and molding social attitudes. For example, such a spiritual orientation will certainly affect our attitudes toward the use of violence, racism, sexism, and other evils.

Today, in both conservative and liberal Christian circles, there is a renewed emphasis on a theocentric model of Christianity that undercuts christocentric spirituality. Some conservative Protestants attempt to reestablish a theocratic ideal in which the example of Jesus as the crucified messiah is not determinative for Christian social ethics. The Jesus figure is melded into the Trinity as divine self-sacrifice, which exalts him as divine judge and sovereign. In liberal circles "theocentric" often indicates an overarching religious ideal that includes and embraces the disparate and even conflicting claims and values of the world's religions, so that Jesus becomes merely one relative expression among many others of the "trinitarian" God. In such a climate the Anabaptist insistence on the normative centrality of Christ as the crucified and resurrected Jesus has enduring relevance.

A Spirituality of Obedience

The spirituality of the Anabaptists marked a significant shift in theological orientation. It was not, as Luther feared, a restatement of works spirituality. It began and ended with grace, but it understood the gracious work of the Savior as enlightenment and enablement. Thus it shifted the focus of theology and the Christian life to what liberation theologians call *praxis*. Further, it insisted that faithful praxis—following the way of Christ—was fundamental to understanding the word of Christ. In his "Hermeneutics and Discipleship" C. J. Dyck notes that there is a correlation in Anabaptist writings between obedience and right understanding of Scripture. "Knowing and doing," he writes, "became a reciprocal experience of understanding and obedience, obedience and understanding."[11]

True Christian spirituality, the Anabaptists held, focused neither on sacraments and meritorious works nor on sacramental grace alone. The mystical element was, in fact, largely eliminated—perhaps excessively so. On the other hand Anabaptist spirituality was not an intellectual spirituality focused on dogma or correct belief. Rather, it was an ethical spirituality centered on the cruciality of right action. Theology and mystical relationship in the Christian life had one major goal: obedient faith.

Since salvation means both justification and renewal of humans in the image of God, true faith can only be expressed in faithful obedience. Indeed, the "image of God" is the image of "true righteousness and holiness" (Eph. 4:24). True spirituality is to know the will of God and by the Spirit's enablement to do it. Of course such doing is in human weakness, as Menno put it. There is no perfection in this life. But there is also no excuse or substitute for the sincere desire to know and do God's will according to the example of Christ, and such a posture of obedience is essential for Spirit inspired hermeneutical practice.

Luther's famous aphorism, "The just [Christian] shall live *by faith*" is well known. Menno Simon's phrasing of this statement is less well known, but it sums up Anabaptist spirituality with precision. In "True

Christian Faith" he wrote that "the just [Christians] must *live their faith*."[12] True faith is faithful obedience.

It was this insistence upon obedience that made the Anabaptists radical Christians. They criticized proponents of magisterial reform for not carrying through with their biblical and theological insights, and disparaged their theological glosses on Scripture that allowed professed Christians to evade obedience. They pleaded with their opponent to give them a clear word from Scripture and promised to obey it. Of course they themselves were sometimes naively literal in their interpretations and faulty in their application of Scripture. But a single-minded insistence on decision and action characterizes their faith. The essence of social and spiritual radicality is the demand for action, and this was the essence of Anabaptist spirituality.

This christocentric spirituality of faithful praxis gives Anabaptism both its challenge and relevance for the twenty-first century. Spiritualities of mystical experience, therapeutic affirmation, theological speculation, or charismatic revelations that claim to link the individual with transcendent reality are currently popular. But it is the deed that will judge us. Jesus' question, "Why do you call me 'Lord' and do not the things that I say?" continues to haunt us.

A Spirituality of the First Beatitude

Several historians have emphasized the monastic backgrounds of some Anabaptist leaders. Others have pointed to the influence on Anabaptism from movements like the Franciscan Tertiaries and the Brethren of the Common Life. However, the close association of the Anabaptist and Peasants movements likely conditioned their attitudes toward poverty more than such influences. The masses of Anabaptists belonged to the peasant and artisan classes, and thus were in solidarity with those oppressed by economic and class stratification. For leaders like Grebel, Marpeck, and Simons, who did not come from the peasant class, poverty meant a conscious decision to join the poor flock of God and minister in their behalf.

Among the Anabaptists, poverty was not a moral ideal as in monasticism, but an existential necessity of the movement. One chose poverty not for the virtue of being poor but as a present means to an eschatological goal.[13] Thus poverty is associated with the cross and suffering for the sake of the kingdom of God.

The persecuted Anabaptists were themselves the "poor." Poverty was not a spiritualized virtue. A decision to join the movement inevitably meant the renunciation of affluence as a goal in life. To enter the kingdom meant literally giving up security, property, and family. By the same token radical sharing and burden bearing were not spiritualized.

When new members were "re"-baptized they entered a community of "those who knew they were poor" (Matt. 5:3, NEB), and mutual burden bearing became a way of survival. To live in solidarity as "the poor" meant sharing the substance of life in their poverty. While not all Anabaptists practiced community of goods, they all insisted on radical sharing as a part of the gospel.

Modern Western affluence based on entrepreneurial prowess and a consumer-driven economy militates against such spirituality. Most "Anabaptists" of the "First World" are willy-nilly the affluent recipients of this unjust economic system, and those who lay claim to the Anabaptist tradition need to find ways to separate themselves from the economic ideology that continues to repress and debilitate the world's poor. Genuine identity with the poor will not allow us to continue to live in affluence unaffected by their plight. The gospel, as our Roman Catholic brothers and sisters have observed, requires us to acknowledge a "preferential option for the poor." As Ron Sider continues to remind us, "Those who neglect the poor and oppressed are not really God's people at all—no matter how frequent their religious rituals or how orthodox their creeds and confessions."[14]

If Anabaptist spirituality is to live and flourish in the twenty-first century, we will have to deal far more radically with this spirituality of poverty. We have thought of persecution as a condition thrust on us from outside and of the accompanying poverty as a condition to be overcome by honest living and hard work. Affluence and institutional power have remained our goal. We have made benevolence or charity a virtue rather than justice and equity. But widespread devastating poverty will never be resolved by charity alone.

A Spirituality of Nonviolent Confrontation

Anabaptism demands a decision. That is the meaning of believers baptism—a decision to change (*metanoia*) and to take a public stand. The act of "re"-baptism was itself a confrontation with the culture in which both baptizer and baptized had been socialized. In like manner, refusal to take a civil oath and to serve in the militia were political as well as religious acts of nonviolent noncooperation with the established civil order. Such a position was in no sense escapist or an act of withdrawal from social responsibility.

This spirit of confrontation was reflected in the understanding of the church as an alternative social order in tension with the civil order. The church was not to be a sectarian city removed to the distant hills to shine as a light. That kind of sectarian stance was a forced option in Anabaptism's ensuing history. The original option was to be salt and light amid society. Nonconformity did not mean a pious, nonresistant separation unto God, but a nonviolent noncooperative confrontation with the injustice and unrighteousness in the existing society.

For many years we in the Anabaptist and Pietist traditions have used nonresistance and nonconformity as excuses for noninvolvement. We substituted sectarian withdrawal for the confrontative alternative community of the Spirit amid the world. More recently it seems that we have become so obsessed with escaping a sectarian image and rejoining the majority culture that we have seriously eroded the necessary tension between the church and the world. Is irresponsible sectarian withdrawal being exchanged for irresponsible compromise and appeasement? Professionalism, eagerness to be identified with the civic community, and a desire to enjoy the fruits of economic success tempt contemporary pietistic Anabaptist congregations to turn a myopic eye and deaf ear to the evils of racism, sexism, poverty, and greed.

The challenge of Anabaptist spirituality for the twenty-first century is to maintain a clear definition of the church as a distinct secular alternative to the violence and injustice of the dominant social order. The church is not to be a religious community insulated or withdrawn from the surrounding culture, which provides its matrix, but a "sectarian" community in the sense that it is in dynamic, confrontative tension with the evils of that society.

The Anabaptists not only confronted the world; they confronted each other in the church. Indeed, as social historians have pointed out, there was a great deal of dissonance and controversy within the group itself. With full admission of their human frailties, however, one must point out the positive side of this conflict.

Confrontation does not necessarily connote animosity and dissension. It does indicate self-awareness, honesty, and energetic participation. It may also evince passionate caring, as in the title of David Augsburger's well-known book, "caring enough to confront." The appeal for hermeneutical dialogue both within and outside the community is based upon this principle. Not only did the Anabaptists call for public disputations with opponents to settle hermeneutical issues; they practiced face-to-face exchange within and among the congregations.[15]

Unfortunately such confrontative dialogue was not always nonviolent, as the many schisms indicate. The sixteenth century was an argumentative age. We may hope that in a more pluralistic age we can learn to make such confrontation, while nonetheless serious, more dialogical than argumentative.

A Gemeinutzlich *Spirituality*

This spirituality of nonviolent confrontation reflects a new sense of individuality emerging in the sixteenth century. The task of our Anabaptist forebears was to *maintain* a viable Christian community in light of the centrifugal forces that were tearing apart the unity of Christendom. While they refused to follow the coercive example of the magisterial reformers who also wrestled with this problem, nevertheless, in the pandemonium of the Reformation, Anabaptism emerged as a radical community of discourse and action. It was by no means a community in full agreement, but it was united in dissatisfaction with the traditional order and concerned about the same issues.[16]

Today in the West we are again witnessing the disintegration of traditional forms of human community such as the family, town hall, and university. Individuality has gone to seed in rampant contemporary individualism. Authoritarian communalism is hardly our protagonist. We face the task of *regathering* a viable Christian community of self-aware individuals into a genuine community of discernment and action.

In the sixteenth century a community of individuals discerning and applying the meaning of Scripture was a freeing experience. It signaled freedom from the hierarchical patriarchy of the Roman Church. It presupposed the impregnation of lay Christians with the Holy Spirit and their empowerment for decision making. Its intended goal was a community of responsible individuals participating in the discernment process and freely endorsing the group consensus.

The cultural ideology of individualism dominates us today. We are jealous of our individual autonomy—our right to self-determination.

We find it difficult even to conceive that self-fulfillment might be found in committed participation and submission to group discernment and consensus (*Gelassenheit*). The group is for the affirmation of our individual egos.

By contrast, loyalty to and the mutual support of one another reinforced the Anabaptist communities of discernment and consensus. While not all Anabaptists agreed on the communal ideal, in the words of John Oyer, they pursued "a community life in which the sharing of material goods was the accepted practice."[17] Even those not practicing "community of goods" did not idealize "the sacred right of private property." They espoused a *gemeinutzlich* spirituality in contrast to an *eigenutzlic* demeanor (a group-service versus self-serving spirit). We might refer to it as a spirituality of *koinonia.*

They comprised a visible "community of saints" rather than an invisible spiritual "communion of saints." While they did not directly participate in the political community, this characteristic gave a social dimension to their spirituality that later pietistic strains of Mennonite sectarianism often lacked.

It is at the point of its *Gemeinde/sectarian* character that the pietistic Anabaptist tradition is most seriously challenged today. Is the Gemeinde (communal) ideal simply a sociological type in the sect cycle? Or is it perhaps essential to the eschatological mission of the church? If the latter, then we should promote a socially responsible model of sectarianism. We should not advocate or expect the completion of the sect cycle until the eschatological consummation.

Earlier we mentioned Bender's concern to articulate a viable denominational vision, which we have come to identify as an Anabaptist-Mennonite ideal type. This institutional vision was to replace the predenominational sectarian peoplehood indicated by the single designation Mennonite. The hyphenated label indicates its denominational character. Of course we need institutional identities to embody the Anabaptist spirit, but what shape might they take? Can the denomination as a social institutional form sufficiently embody a Gemeinde spirituality to qualify as genuinely Anabaptist in its present pluralistic form? Should we try to preserve the denominational structure or search for other ways to embody the characteristics of gemeinutzlich spirituality.

American Mennonite denominations from the "Old Orders" to the latest fundamentalist versions have become so pluralistic and diluted with "Americanity" that a major regrouping may be necessary in this century if Gemeinde spirituality is to survive. Can the denominational form be redefined and reorganized to be a viable expression of biblical values and spirituality as embodied in the Anabaptist tradition? Or will it simply follow the pattern of mainline denominations with only the preservation of a few ethnic cultural idiosyncrasies? This is the challenge that faces us as a cluster of related Mennonite and Brethren denominations.

Notes

1. Recent historical studies seem to have shown conclusively that there never was a generation of pristine Anabaptists, including the first, who fully embodied the vision. See Werner Packull, *Mysticism and the Early South-German-Austrian Anabaptist Movement* (Scottdale, Pa.: Herald Press, 1990), 11.

2. "Authority was more Scripture than Spirit, though it was hardly an either-or issue for them." *Lutheran Reformers Against Anabaptists* (The Hague: Martinus Nijhof, 1964), 230, also 164-65. Cf. J. Denny Weaver's conclusions in his doctoral dissertation, "The Doctrine of God, Spirit and Word in Early Anabaptist Theology 1522-1530" (Duke University, 1974).

3. "Between Paradigms: Anabaptist Studies at the Crossroads," *The Conrad Grebel Review* 8 (Winter 1990) 9-10. Packull takes his clues from Peter Bickle's characterization of Anabaptism as a "*Gemeinde-reformation*" and Walter Klaassen's "*Gemeinde theologie.*"

4. "The Anabaptist Vision and Social Justice," in *Freedom and Discipleship: Liberation Theology in an Anabaptist Perspective*, ed. Daniel Schipani (Maryknoll: Orbis Press, 1989), 108-109.

5. Oyer, 90-91. Calvin Redekop has surveyed the various views of scholars on the subject of the Anabaptist essence and ranked the elements according to their frequency. He then proposes a taxonomy of his own based upon this data. See "The Community of Scholars and the Essence of Anabaptism," *Mennonite Quarterly Review* 67(October 1993): 429ff.

6. "Between Paradigms," 22.

7. Arnold Snyder points out that Sattler's christocentrism distinguishes him from the original Zurich group and most probably represents the influence of his Benedictine background. The Benedictine rule, he writes, was christocentric. "Christocentric" in this sense of *Nachfolge*, then, is differentiated from "christological," which denotes a more theological import. See *The Life and Thought of Michael Sattler* (Scottdale, Pa.: Herald Press, 1984).

8. H. Wayne Pipkin and John H. Yoder, trans. and eds., *Balthasar Hubmaier: Theologian of Anabaptism* (Scottdale, Pa.: Herald Press, 1989), 468.

9. Kenneth Davis, *Anabaptism and Asceticism* (Scottdale, Pa.: Herald Press, 1974). 177.

10. Ibid., 170ff. Cf. Robert Friedmann's article, "*Gelassenheit*," in the *Mennonite Encyclopedia*, vol. 2 (Scottdale, Pa.: Herald Press, 1956), 449. He ends by saying, "Present-day Mennonitism has lost the idea of Gelassenheit nearly completely; yet with the recovery of the ideal of discipleship also Gelassenheit may be revived."

11. See Willard Swartley, ed., *Essays on Biblical Interpretation: Anabaptist-Mennonite Perspectives* (Elkhart: Institute of Mennonite Studies, 1984), 30, 37.

12. *The Complete Writings of Menno Simons*, ed. John C. Wenger (Scottdale, Pa.: Herald Press, 1956), 309.

13. As Santa Ana writes, "For the Christian poverty and existence of the poor in this world are a scandal, which is why the kingdom is promised to them to change their condition"; *Good News to the Poor* (Maryknoll: Orbis Press, 1979), 101.

14. Ronald J. Sider, "Mennonites and the Poor: Toward an Anabaptist Theology of Liberation," in Schipani, *Freedom and Discipleship*, 95.

15. Adolph Ens points out the significance of the Anabaptists' call for public disputations to determine the meaning and use of Scripture in his "The Anabaptist Hermeneutic Community," *The Church as Theological Community*, ed. Harry Huebner (Winnipeg: Canadian Mennonite Bible College, 1990), 69-89

16. John Roth, following a lead by David Sabean, suggests that the community (*Gemeinde*) of sixteenth-century Anabaptism cannot be described as an "ideal type." Rather, it is defined by a common "discourse," "argument," or "*raisonnement*." See his paper, "Anabaptist Uses of Scripture," read at the Bridgewater Conference on Anabaptism, 1993.

17. Oyer, 90.

8

Spirit and Spirituality: Reclaiming Biblical Transcendence

Parachurch, pre-evangelism—in the 1960s and 1970s, words such as these became common parlance in evangelical circles. In addition to being popularly disseminated and widely embraced, the terms manifested a concept of the church and its mission based on a clear division between the spiritual realm, which implied a supernatural reality, and the natural realm, which included the physical, psychological, and social dimensions of life. Most evangelical leaders in these years still championed dualistic supernaturalism, which Princeton theologian B. B. Warfield had decades earlier dubbed the life-breath of orthodox Christianity.[1] In this rendering of the faith, *the gospel* was a strictly "spiritual" message that called for "supernatural" rebirth. Correspondingly, *salvation* was defined as a spiritual and theological transaction apart from which *social service* was humanistic busy work. For these evangelicals, the true mission of the church was evangelism, i.e., calling people to belief. Attempts to express New Testament *agape* in social terms could only be justified as "*pre*-evangelism."[2]

Although the evangelical movement, broadly defined, has moved beyond this point, the issue remains a source of tension. For example, Franklin Graham's careful distinction between the *spiritual* and the *social* activities of his relief organization, Samaritan's Purse, and his insistence on verbal apologetics against Islam, highlight the tension. Even popular magazines have homed in on this dilemma, particularly as it pertains to the presence of Christian missionaries in societies that have made proselytizing illegal.[3] What does it mean to evangelize Muslims? How is the "secular humanitarian team" of an evangelical missions organization related to its goal of evangelism? Is "non-proselytizing material aid" a sufficient Christian witness? Or must it be "aid plus gospel?" How is "relationship evangelism" related to "saving souls?" Clearly the theological definitions underlying the Church's missional philosophy need careful evaluation and, in some cases, considerable rethinking.

Spirit and Flesh

Conceptualizing the relationship between the spiritual and the physical/material has been a persistent challenge in Western thought. The problem is already reflected in the New Testament, which adopts the language of the Greek ethos to continue the salvation story of the Hebrew Scriptures. With the continuing shift in the church's early centuries from implicit Hebraic assumptions to Neoplatonic dualism, the spirit-flesh question became especially focused in Christian theological discussions.

In the Hebrew tradition, the transcendence of the spiritual realm was not infinitely separated from the earthly realm. God the invisible Sovereign Spirit (*ruach*) ruled both the invisible and visible realms, which were part of one total reality or universe. Humanity was created in God's *image* and made to partake in God's ruach. In other words, God was transcendent Creator, the *independent* Sovereign of the universe, who granted humanity *dependent* creaturely life to serve as co-regents over the earth. The heavens, which were beyond human control, were God's domain—the bridge between the visible and invisible, as it were. God dwelt beyond the outermost reaches of the visible realm but nevertheless in the universe. God dwelt in eternity, but eternity was nonetheless conceived as the extension of time.

The implications of this paradigm for understanding the relationship between spirit and flesh should be obvious. While acknowledging two dimensions of reality—transcendent and earthly, invisible and visible, independent and dependent, spirit and flesh—the Hebrew framework represented an organic continuum of being. Humanity in all of its sentient aspects—physical, psychological, social, political, intellectual, and emotional—was resonant with spiritual being. Flesh was considered an embodiment of the vital spirit that was manifest in both creaturely being (*nephesh*) and the ultimate Creator-God.

This Hebrew paradigm stood in sharp contrast to the philosophical dualism that, in various ways, influenced early Christian conceptions of flesh and spirit. Greek dualism conceptualized the spirit and the flesh as infinitely discrete substances. According to a view that we might call "infinite transcendence," the ultimate source of being was beyond being. According to Neoplatonic thought, a series of theoretical emanations were needed to bridge the infinite divide between Ultimate Spiritual Unity and a divine being called the Demiurge, who created the flawed world of matter that humans actually experience.

Therefore, when the Neoplatonists thought of spirit with respect to humanity, they pictured it as a spark of the divine on loan from the creative spirit. They conceived spirit not as a gestalt or image in which human beings had been created, but rather as a spirit or soul that was trapped prison-like in a physical body. They thus reified spirit as a highly refined substance that intermingled with the flesh, and they deemed the flesh (animal body) to be evil or at least a lesser, corruptible good—the source of temptation to the spirit that should be ignored, destructively indulged, or vigorously disciplined. In sum, the Neoplationists associated the spiritual life with the mind (*nous*) and its refined intellectual activity, and they devalued physical and societal activity as an unavoidable consequence of the fleshly body and its needs. Salvation, in this view, was reduced to an escape of the spirit from its fleshly entrapment.

Already in the second century some Christians had adopted this dualistic paradigm and had consequently defined true spirituality as detachment from the material-social world. The goal of Gnostic Christian spirituality, writes Robert Grant, was escaping to "the world infinitely remote and infinitely close because [it was] attainable within oneself."[4] Thus, according to the Gnostics, the truly spiritual person lived a life of detachment from the material-physical and social aspects of life. Under the influence of Neoplatonism, Christian leaders like Origen defined spirituality in intellectual and mystical terms, and they championed asceticism and martyrdom as the purist type of spirituality.

Given this philosophical framework, it is hardly surprising that early Christian theologians considered virginity, i.e., a life of sexual continence, the epitome of Christian spirituality. What we often miss, however, are the broader social implications of such virginity as the highest expression of spirituality. Virginity was not primarily a moral rejection of sexuality, but rather the renunciation of the fleshly, human society based on marriage and family ties. According to Peter Brown, sexual intercourse constituted "the necessary act on which the solidarity and perpetuity of the human race depended." The monasteries and convents were seen as alternative spiritual societies bonded in "angelic" solidarity, not flesh and blood. They were, Brown observes, "an exact imitation on earth of the 'life of the angels'."[5]

Furthermore, many early Christians understood virginity as a form of mediation between God and humanity. Extrapolating from Christ's virgin birth and Mary's exaltation to divinity, Gregory of Nyssa wrote that "virginity has become the linking force that assures the intimacy of human beings with God."[6] It was both a condition and expression of ultimate spirituality. Celibate life in monastic community was thus considered the highest form of Christian spirituality. This model of spirituality, so dominant in the church for fifteen hundred years, identified spirituality with renunciation of temporal vocations and natural social relationships. And with the secularization of the temporal and natural, the gap between the spiritual and the secular became even more pronounced.

This dualism played itself out in many ways in the church's history. For instance, the governance of Christendom was soon divided between the spiritual and temporal realms, temporal meaning social-political. Within this dualistic framework, *religious* was understood as the sphere of spiritual vocation and *secular* was understood as the sphere of natural giftedness. The clergy thus assumed sacramental spiritual power, and the secular laity did little but receive their spiritual services. In the church's ethical reflection, numerous Christian thinkers drew a qualitative line between the spiritual virtue of agape love and secular virtue of social justice. More recently, many Christians have drawn a stark distinction between spiritual ministry and the humanitarian professions, and between evangelism and social service. And in the personal lives of Christians, popular theologians have distinguished between sanctification and self-discipline, between Holy Spirit-inspired "gifts" and natural human compassion.

North American Developments

A brief look at some twentieth-century theological developments confirms the lingering effects of theological dualism in North American evangelical theology. These years, historians tell us, exhibited a strong and sustained conservative reaction to the threat of rational empiricism, often referred to as liberalism. While many conservative theologians participated in this battle, few were as widely read or as influential as Lewis Sperry Chafer, who founded Dallas Theological Seminary in 1924 and taught there until his death in 1952. Chafer is perhaps best known for organizing the work of the Plymouth Brethren and C. I. Scofield into an eight-volume theological work.[7] But in addition to his systematic theology, Chafer published numerous other books, one of which—*He That Is Spiritual*, released in 1918—is particularly relevant for our purposes, for it quickly became a definitive text for conservative dispensationalists who dominated America's fundamentalist movement for most of the twentieth century.

Dispensationalism itself was not Chafer's invention, but rather had its origins in Great Britain's Darbyite (Plymouth Brethren) movement. An eschatological scheme that divided Christian history into seven distinct eras (dispensations), dispensationalism significantly impacted theology in the United States through the teaching of the Plymouth Brethren following the War Between the States.[8] Men like D. L. Moody and A. T. Pierson, who played significant roles in the promotion of Protestant missions, were much influenced by the Brethren. More recently, Billy Graham commented appreciatively that evangelicals have all milked the Plymouth Brethren cow.

Although dispensationalism is best known for its eschatological claims, it is most significant for our purposes to note that the Plymouth Brethren made an ontological distinction between the spiritual world and the empirical, material world, creating a sharply dualistic understanding of the created order. Humans, they believed, were made of distinct entities: body, soul, and spirit. The Brethren made a similarly sharp distinction between the church as spiritual body and as a social organization (denomination), and between the spiritual life and social life of the individual. They understood the Bible to be the inerrant (supernatural) words of God, thus identifying spirituality with a strict biblical literalism, and they defined salvation as a supernatural spiritual rebirth (regeneration) that was distinct from any renewal of the soul (rational faculty) or healing of the body. According to the Brethren, the single vocation of the church was to rescue souls from hellfire—in their words, to "snatch them from the burning"—and call them to a higher spirituality.

Working within these parameters, Chafer sought to define spirituality. In contrast to liberal concepts of the spiritual as "human potential"[9] and, at the other pole, the Pentecostals' concept of the spiritual as an ecstatic empirical experience, Chafer defined spirituality as a strictly theological virtue.[10] He insisted that Christian spirituality was a supernatural gift of the Holy Spirit received by faith alone, something quite distinct from human aptitudes or abilities. The most he would grant Pentecostals by way of feeling was "celestial heart-ecstasy," i.e., an inner assurance that God gave spiritual people according to their faith.[11]

Chafer begins his argument in *He That is Spiritual* by drawing an impenetrable line of distinction between the Holy Spirit of God and the human spirit and, from that, between Christian love and human love. The human spirit, says Chafer, is not only creaturely but also depraved. Correspondingly, Christian love, which is inspired by the Spirit of God, "may be manifested in a human life" but should never be confused with human love.[12] Supernaturally gifted love is the only basis for Christian virtue; human love, on the other hand, is the source of humanitarianism and humanism.

Building on this particular understanding of love, Chafer was able to define true spirituality as the "direct manifestation of the Spirit" and to claim further that each true Christian had a "foreordained" spiritual service that could only be known by those yielded to the Spirit.[13] Chafer's distinction between spiritual and unspiritual Christians is particularly clear in the following claim: "Any Christian may enter into his own 'good works,' since the enabling Spirit is already indwelling him; but only those do enter in who are yielded to God; for it is service according to *His* will."[14] In sum, the secret of genuine spirituality is "total yieldedness" to the Spirit. For Chafer, then, spirituality is virtually equated with what Andrew Murray called "absolute surrender," or walking in the Spirit.[15] Apart from this yieldedness, service and ministry are "fleshly undertakings."

This brand of spirituality, it must be noted, is purely inward. Its only empirical sign is "true Christian character," not "works."[16] Authentic spiritual "works" are "gifts of the Spirit," not the result of "natural ability," and there is no one kind of work that can be used as a test of spirituality (though "intercessory prayer" is the greatest ministry a spirit-filled Christian can engage in). When we consider these claims, and add to them the fundamentalists' suspicion of any kind of "social work," we can easily see how spirituality and social justice work became disconnected in Fundamentalism by their very definition!

To summarize, this pattern of spirituality—epitomized by Chafer and still predominant in much of contemporary conservative North American Christianity—begins with the concept of spirit as one discrete part of the human being: "spirit, soul, and body." It defines spirituality as giving priority to the spiritual in contrast to the rational (soul) or fleshly (body). Identifying the spirit with the interior aspects of life, it emphasizes inwardness, subjectivity, and the inner life. And it focuses on the ecstatic experience in contrast to the rational; on God-awareness and self-understanding in contrast to ethical action; on transformation of the self into a spiritual rather than a rational or materialistic person. Such spirituality manifests itself in personal expressions of piety, submission to God, unquestioning belief in the Bible, expressions of joy in the face of disappointment, and trust in the face of difficulty. It is an end in itself.

From Secularity to Secularism

Chafer and his theologically like-minded friends were not operating in a vacuum. The contemporary secularist paradigm they found so problematic was (and remains) a big part of the problem, for it offered only truncated and rationally constructed categories within which to define theological concepts. Beginning with the rational elimination of a transcendent reality, which its scientific methodology cannot investigate and verify, secularism limited truth to quantifiable scientific data. It equated reality with empirical (sense) experience, classified experience into separate distinct either-or categories, and progressed only by means of rational and mathematical speculation based on inductive research. All of this, as we know, has been very productive for the advance of empirical knowledge, but it has proved quite inadequate for religious and moral evaluation.

Unfortunately, the Liberal-Fundamentalist debates of the twentieth century's first half proceeded largely along these lines, with Fundamentalism readily adopting the rational and dualistic categories of natural-supernatural, knowledge-belief, individual-communal, Spirit-led-humanistic, and spiritual-social in the course of defining and defending its positions. Fundamentalist theologians thus failed to recognize the subtle but crucial difference between what Christopher Kaiser calls "biblical secularity" and contemporary secularism, an oversight that led them to make unnecessary ontological distinctions between the spiritual and the social.[17] Today's post-fundamentalist evangelicals continue to be plagued by this semantic confusion, even though Kaiser's distinction provides them and others with a meaningful way out.

In "biblical secularity,"[18] Kaiser explains, God and spirit are integrally, even ontologically, related to the secular process of historical development. Heaven is part of what we today call the universe; God is king, directing the political life of the nation; and charismatic servants, judges, and prophets carry out God's purposes in the political life of the nation. Even angels serve as agents in the historical process, for while they may be invisible, they are nonetheless real, thus belonging to the realm of the *secular*, i.e., the reality of this age.

According to this biblically informed understanding of reality, God's spiritual laws regulate the political society, and social ethics are matters of spirituality. Economic and juridical justice, agricultural practice, and military strategy (along with temple ritual and individual worship) are matters of one's personal relationship with and responsibility before God. Since the theocratic rule of Yahweh marks out the parameters of spirituality, it would be strange, if not unthinkable, to separate spirituality and social justice. As Paul observed in Rom 14:17, the kingdom of God (a spiritual reality) is a "matter of righteousness [justice as a personal-social ethic] and peace and joy in the Holy Spirit." Notice how naturally these fit together!

In contrast, the contemporary Western division of the sacred and the secular effectively separates these realms. In the historical process we know as secularization, the natural was first separated from the supernatural, then public social life from individual private life. Instead of nature and supernature being dimensions within a wholistic environment, they became two separate spheres. The supernatural (nonempirical or spiritual) was relegated to the individual (the private, subjective sphere), and the social or public sphere was secularized.

All of this had significant consequences for the nature and mission of the church, for the church quickly became associated (in many Christian's minds) with the supernatural realm, and its primary work was deemed to be spiritual in nature. Especially in the United States, where constitutional law separates church and state, the church became identified with the individual private sphere. This, of course, was not true of John Calvin's reform, nor was it true of Wesleyan holiness with its emphasis on sanctification (even though John Wesley himself operated within a dualistic paradigm). But since the early twentieth century, American Christianity in general and evangelicals in particular have been beset by this radical disparity of the two realms.

Early twentieth-century fundamentalists exemplified this problem most clearly, for they subjectivized the spiritual and separated themselves from the public order, thus functionalizing the rift between social and spiritual. Moreover, fundamentalists individualized the meaning of person, reducing it to an individual-in-private capacity. With respect to the work of the church, they defined gospel as a purely spiritual message and evangelism as the verbal proclamation of that message. Not surprisingly, they designated church professions "spiritual" and branded professions like law, medicine, teaching, and social work "secular," even if practiced by Christians.

The fundamentalists' divide between the spiritual and the secular even had consequences for their apologetic work. In their well-intentioned attempt to contextualize biblical terminology, many fundamentalist theologians embraced empirical definitions of modern secularism to explain biblical narratives and teachings. For instance, they defined biblical miracle as an empirical category; that is, the spiritual phenomena reported in the Bible as publicly attested acts of God (miracles) were understood to be empirical, historical events caused by supernatural powers that interrupted natural causation.[19] Many of these theologians argued that, with the end of the apostolic writings (which they considered miraculous revelation in the sense identified above), such miracles ceased. They henceforth made a theological distinction between the natural and the supernatural, the temporal and the spiritual, whether or not any empirical distinction could actually be observed.

For our purposes it is most significant to note that the acceptance of this rationalistic paradigm further reinforced the schism between the spiritual and the historical-social. Those who embraced this paradigm limited the miraculous to the experience of personal salvation—understood as a private, individual, subjective event that, strictly speaking, could only be believed and confessed.[20] Correspondingly, they classified social acts of compassion and justice as humanitarian good works and disregarded them as necessary aspects of authentic spirituality. In other words, they considered social action, however good and desirable, to be secular or humanistic apart from the miracle of spiritual new birth. For them, professed intellectual belief and verbal confession of receiving Christ—more than a distinguishable lifestyle or a compassionate mode of living—constituted the evidence of spiritual renewal. Consequently, they deemed laboring for the miraculous salvation of the world to be the church's primary work, a mission accomplished by preaching and prayer. The social gospel was, in their rendering, an ersatz humanitarian gospel because it did not manifest the definable spiritual characteristics.

The Paradigm Shift

At least since the publication of Carl F. H. Henry's *The Uneasy Conscience of Modern Fundamentalism* (1947), evangelical leaders have been cognizant of the problem evangelicals have had in integrating spiritual ministry and social service. Fundamentalist churches, of course, had long encouraged philanthropic activity (e.g., charitable relief) to accompany their evangelistic work, but they nonetheless considered denominational social service programs suspect. Henry decried Fundamentalism's "embarrassing divorce from a world social program," and he called for a renewed fundamentalism to compete on the world scene as "a vital world ideology . . . project[ing] a solution for the world's most pressing problems."[21]

Still, Henry saw "no need for Fundamentalism to embrace liberalism's defunct social gospel,"[22] and instead based his strategy, which he labeled "supernatural redemptionism," on the uncompromising assumptions of dualistic supernaturalism.[23] In fact, Henry built his call for social involvement on a definition of the evangelical task that was entirely within Fundamentalism's traditional understanding of spiritual priorities. "The evangelical task primarily," wrote Henry, "is the preaching of the gospel, in the interest of individual regeneration by the supernatural grace of God, in such a way that divine redemption can be recognized as the best solution of our problems, individual and social."[24]

This priority continues to be the identifying characteristic of the evangelical movement.[25] In the 1960s and 1970s, evangelical parachurch organizations like World Vision were rationalized as "pre-evangelism," and more wholistic programs like the Sojourners community remained on the margins of the movement. In the 1970s and 1980s,

John R. W. Stott enunciated what Nancey Murphy has since called "holistic dualism"[26] and was instrumental in persuading most evangelicals that an integrated social service and spiritual witness were essential to the expression of genuine Christian agape. Nevertheless, Stott continued to use the *both* (evangelism)-*and* (social service) terminology of traditional dualistic theology. Similarly, contemporary evangelical social programs like Ronald J. Sider's Evangelicals for Social Action and Franklin Graham's Samaritan's Purse are embraced as legitimate *evangelistic strategies* under the traditional slogan "evangelism *and* social service."

This both-and rationale reveals an inherent ambivalence and implies a need to strike a proper "balance" between two aspects of wholistic Christian ministry, namely, verbal presentation and active demonstration of the gospel. By implication it forces an ideological judgment about the relative importance of social ministry and evangelism. Granted, sociologist James Davison Hunter reports a growing conviction among evangelical college and seminary students that social ministry has an "intrinsic worth . . . *apart from* [sic] ultimate spiritual concern."[27] But while Hunter's finding may be welcomed as recognition of social ministry as a distinctly Christian responsibility, the rhetorical separation of these two values—"intrinsic worth" and "spiritual concern"—signals the problem inherent in a dualistic theological rationale. To the contrary, the intrinsic worth of social ministry stems from the spiritual reality and value of human life as affirmed in Christ. It is precisely participation in the ministry of Christ through the dynamic of his Spirit that gives secular ministry intrinsic worth. To be sure, institutional priorities need to be defined and ministries distinguished for practical purposes, but the theological rationale undergirding and guiding Christian ministry should always be unitive.

It is therefore my contention that locating an adequate theological rationale for wholistic spiritual service requires a paradigm shift that begins with our very conception of spirit and spirituality. The modified dualism of evangelical theologians still leaves us with an ideological contrast that requires a choice of priorities and a need to "balance" Christian ministries. As long as spirit (*pneuma*) is identified solely with eternal being—immortality, infinity, perfection—in contrast to body (*sarks*), which is physical, temporal, finite, and corruptible, the recognition of humans as wholistic, personal creatures in God's image will remain elusive. So, too, will a wholistic Christian ministry to the body (*soma*, which includes the dimension of spirit).

This paradigm shift will require, at the very least, a basic redefinition of divine immanence and transcendence and a more nuanced distinction between biblical secularity and modern secularism. The older dualism between the spiritual and the temporal inherited from the Greeks will need to give way to a more wholistic (*pneumo-somatic*) view of human reality. Beginning already in the mid-twentieth century, some philosophers and theologians (who are sometimes referred to as "neo-classical") began to probe the possibilities of a more careful statement of God's relation to the universe of matter. In the interest of defending theism against the criticism of secular rationalism, they began to use terms such as "dipolar" and "panentheistic" to describe God's relation to the created universe.[28]

More recently, Roman Catholic theologian David Tracy has advocated this same term. In an interview with the *Christian Century*, Tracy argued that "panentheism, the doctrine that all is in God but God's inclusion of the world does not exhaust the reality of God, is the best way to render in contemporary concepts God's relationship to us as described in the Bible."[29] Whatever philosophical term we use, it seems obvious that we need to re-image God's relationship to the world and humankind. The use of Neoplatonic categories of transcendence as it has played out in contemporary rational empiricism does not adequately represent "biblical secularity."

By the same token, and as part of the shift, Christians will need to revise their conception of *humans in the image of God*. Theologian Nancey Murphy, who has used terms like "holistic dualism" to describe "the most common position in church history, at least from Augustine to the present century," proposes a more precise term like "nonreductive physicalism" to describe and contextualize the biblical understanding of humanity.[30] Murphy argues, both for theological and scientific reasons, that "there is only one entity, the *person*, who is clearly a physical, biological organism," and that "such an organism is indeed capable of all of those higher human capacities that have been attributed to the soul."[31] It is precisely this creature "in the image of God" that can recognize the voice of God and respond to God's will for the world.[32]

I therefore propose a theological conception of spirituality that begins with spirit as a *dimension* of the total human being created in God's image, not as a *distinct part* in conflict or even in tension with the rational soul and the physical body.[33] Too often Christians have substituted the Stoic concept of the image as a "divine spark" *in* human beings for the biblical image of "human beings *in* the image of God," thus equating the *imago Dei* with some faculty or part of the human being (e.g., Stoic reason or Gnostic spirit) in exclusion of the physical body. The implication of the Genesis conception of human beings in all their physicality, including sexual identity, seems to have eluded us.

To more adequately integrate the christocentric spiritual experience and its social expression, contemporary Christians will need to think outside the old dualistic parameters of faith and works, spiritual and ethical, salvation of souls and reconciliation of persons, private virtue and public action, and agape and justice. Social concepts like biblical righteousness, justice, and holiness must be reconnected to both our concepts of spirituality and salvation. In sum, we will need to reframe the eschatological social vision of salvation as the restoration of the rule of God expressed in Ephesians1:10. Indeed, the very concept the "kingdom of God" as Jesus announced it already conflates the historical-social (secular-temporal) and the spiritual (transcendent-eternal). As Paul writes so eloquently, when the kingdom finally becomes universal reality, then God "will be all and in all" (Rom 15:24). Maranatha!

Summary

The dualistic traditions strongly influenced by Neoplatonism and Gnostic Christianity make personal piety the requisite expression of spirituality and, correspondingly, devalue the spiritual character of social ministry. According to this conception of the Christian life, the fruit of the Spirit in a person's life may provide motivation for social action, but spirituality is not immediately identified with compassionate social action. Instead, spirituality is associated with ascetical, monastic community (in contrast to secular-temporal society), mystical contemplation, devotional piety, evangelistic witness, and charismatic worship.

This theological bifurcation of the spiritual and social-psychological, I have contended, develops almost inevitably from an inadequate conception of the ontological relationship between the historical-temporal (empirical) and the transcendent-eternal (unseen). It is, at its most basic, a consequence of the sharp dualism of the spirit and the material-physical, i.e., a consequence of conceiving of spirit as a distinct aspect of human beings combined with an animal body.

A more adequate conception of Christian spirituality begins with an understanding of the spiritual person as one who experiences life in its totality under the influence of God's enabling presence. In this rendering, one's spiritual character expresses itself in a spirit of compassion and a profound sense of grace. It emphasizes praxis in following the nonviolent way of Jesus, and it strives for God's justice and the coming of God's kingdom (Matt 5:6). In short, it incarnates Micah's call "to do justice, love compassion and walk humbly with God" (Mic. 6:8).

While Christians must never negate the vertical dimension of the Christian life (i.e., the work of the Spirit of God influencing and enabling the Christian life), lived expression must be considered the essential identifying mark of Christian spirituality. Indeed, true spirituality is the fulfillment of the image of God in its full individual and societal gestalt—personal, social, political. That this attainment is the gift of the Creator-Savior God, who is the sustaining spiritual dynamic of life, we freely and thankfully recognize.

Notes

1. In his article entitled "Christian Supernaturalism," first published in 1897, he wrote, "The supernatural is the very breath of Christianity's nostrils." Reprinted in *Biblical and Theological Studies*, ed. Samuel Craig (Philadelphia: Presbyterian and Reformed Publishing Co., 1952), 1-21.

2. This distinction between the natural and the supernatural, between spiritual and psychosomatic realities, between the "personal" and the "social," may have been present in traditional Protestant orthodoxy, but it was exacerbated by the Modernist-Fundamentalist debate in the early twentieth century. In these years, the "social gospel" became an oxymoron for Christian fundamentalists. For them, the church was a spiritual, "heavenly" reality not to be confused with the ecclesiastical institution, and "saving souls" was its business.

3. See, for example, "Missionaries Under Cover," *Time* (June 30, 2003): 36-44.

4. Robert Grant, "Gnostic Spirituality," in *Christian Spirituality: Origins to the Twelfth Century*, ed. Bernard McGinn and John Meyendorff (New York: Crossroad, 1987), 56.

5. Peter Brown, "The Notion of Virginity in the Early Church," in *Christian Spirituality: Origins to the Twelfth Century*, 428, 429.

6. Ibid., 432.

7. Lewis Sperry Chafer, *Systematic Theology*, vols. 1-8 (Dallas, Tex.: Dallas Seminary Press, 1947-1948).

8. C. Norman Kraus, *Dispensationalism in America: Its Rise and Development* (Richmond, Va.: John Knox, 1958).

9. James W. Jones, *The Spirit and the World* (New York: Hawthorn Books, 1975), 148-49.

10. At Explo'72, organized by Youth For Christ at the Dallas Cowboys' stadium, these two perspectives came to an explosive climax when Pentecostals, who had been refused a display booth, entered the grounds with signs reading, "Expose '72." Chafer's perspective was enshrined in the "Four Spiritual Laws" which were promoted at this convention as a superior evangelistic tool.

11. Lewis Sperry Chafer, *He That is Spiritual* (Our Hope Publisher, 1918), 56.

12. Ibid., 44.

13. Ibid., 45-46, 48.

14. Ibid., 49.

15. Andrew Murray (1828-1917) was a Dutch missionary pastor whose writings became popular in conservative pietistic circles. His *Absolute Surrender*, published in London in 1895, was widely used in the United States and continued in print well into the twentieth century.

16. Ibid., 55-56.

17. Christopher Kaiser, "From Biblical Secularity to Modern Secularism: Historical Aspects and Stages," in *The Church Between Gospel and Culture: The Emerging Mission in North America,* ed. George R. Hunsberger and Craig Van Gelder (Grand Rapids, Mich.: Eerdmans, 1996), 79-112. Kaiser's seminal article explains the significant difference between "biblical secularity" and contemporary secularism. I have used his insights todevelop my own description of the subtle but significant ontological difference between biblical concepts of miracles (and the relation of the spiritual realm to history) and modern Fundamentalism's empiricist translation of these concepts.

18. Kaiser explains, "By 'biblical secularity' I mean the positive value placed on time, temporal events, and temporal goals in Holy Scripture. God created the world of space and time as a medium of divine self-expression and self-revelation to humanity. God also gives some space and time to each creature as an opportunity for self-fulfillment and service to others. Therefore, the seasonal times of individual life and the historical times of communal history are viewed in Scripture as being filled with theological significance." Noting the difficulty of defining modern secularism, he writes, "Personally, I am persuaded by scholars like Thomas Luckmann and Peter Berger, who define secularism not as the decline of religion but as a redefinition of its role in such a way that religious beliefs are dissociated from the secular processes of world-structuring, and secular values are alienated from the sphere of religion." Ibid., 79, 82.

19. For example, they interpreted creation as a historical event that could be chronologically located in time, the virgin birth as an empirical exception to genetic processes, and revelation as an empirical communication between God and humans.

20. The Pentecostal movement largely accepted the dispensational hermeneutic of biblical literalism, the separation of the spiritual and social, and the emphasis on individual supernatural salvation. It modified the position, however, by allowing individual ecstatic experience of the Spirit's work to count as evidence of supernatural new birth. This reintroduced the possibility of miracles (speaking in tongues, prophecy,

and healing) as experiential signs of spiritual rebirth and Spirit endowment. In the United States, these signs were rarely social in character. Pentecostals in impoverished cultures have been much more open to the spiritual validity of "gifts" of social services.

21. Carl F. H. Henry, *The Uneasy Conscience of Modern Fundamentalism* (Grand Rapids, Mich.: Eerdmans, 1947), 68, 76.

22. Ibid., 85.

23. The sociopolitical programs of the contemporary Religious Right seem designed to fulfill Henry's challenge, although Henry himself did not champion their causes.

24. Ibid., 88.

25. Sociologist James Davison Hunter notes that, "when asked to choose the most important priority for Christians today, nine out of ten Evangelical seminarians chose priorities of a spiritual nature." Hunter, *Evangelicalism: The Coming Generation* (Chicago: University of Chicago Press, 1987), 41.

26. Nancey C. Murphy, Re*conciling Theology and Science: A Radical Reformation Perspective* (Kitchener, Ont.: Pandora Press, 1997), 36-37, 58-59.

27. Hunter, *Evangelicalism: The Coming Generation*, 45. Emphasis added.

28. Philosophers such as Charles Hartshorne, and theologians like Schubert Ogden, Norman Pittenger, and John Cobb, are associated with this position. In his last volume of theology, Paul Tillich, who was sometimes criticized for being too *pantheistic*, introduced the term "eschatological panentheism" in order to preserve the personal dynamic in the relation of God to the universe. See *Systematic Theology III* (Chicago: University of Chicago Press, 1963), 421. Van A Harvey, in his *Handbook of Theological Terms* (New York: Macmillan, 1964), explains the intended meaning of the term: "Just as a person is both the sum of all his experiences and parts and yet more than they, so God has all the finite being as part of his being and experience but transcends it" (172).

29. David Tracy, "The Impossible God," *Christian Century* (13-20 February 2002): 24. See also David Tracy, *Blessed Rage for Order: The New Pluralism in Theology* (San Francisco: Harper & Row, 1988).

30. Murphy, *Reconciling Theology and Science*, 58-59.

31. Ibid., 59. Emphasis in original.

32. Murphy writes, "I believe nonreductive physicalism is close to the ancient Hebrew conception of the person. It maintains the *holistic* view of the person found in both the Old and New testaments. It has theological advantages over dualism. Most important, it forces us to attend to New Testament teaching about bodily resurrection as the source of Christian hope for eternal life." Ibid., 59.

33. See C. Norman Kraus, *An Intrusive Gospel? Christian Mission in the Postmodern World* (Downers Grove, Ill.: InterVarsity, 1998), 69ff., 84-86.

9

The Primal Temptation—A Technological Fix

Commentators have long recognized that the story of Adam and Eve's temptation in the second and third chapters of Genesis is not primarily a story about the origin of moral awareness and guilt. The tree symbolizing "the knowledge of good and evil" is not knowledge of moral right and wrong, which comes as recognition of guilty disobedience. Unfortunately the *Contemporary English Version* published by the American Bible Society, which on the whole is excellent, still perpetuates this inadequate interpretation.

The point is not simply that for the first time they became morally aware of themselves as bad children. Rather, lured by the promise of technological progress and control of their own destiny, they overstepped their bounds despite God's warning. In doing so they lost their innocence. They discovered to their shame that their disregard of God's warning had uncovered their real vulnerability (nakedness), and that they were under the inevitable warrant of death, not the new possibility of controlling their destiny.

Many different interpretations of the "original sin" have been offered. Some have suggested that the original temptation and sin was sexual enticement and indulgence. Others that it was resentment at the limitation of the taboo that God had issued without explanation. (See my *God Our Savior*, Herald Press, 1991, 126ff.) Few, if any, have related it directly to the dilemma of human technology viewed as the solution to the human problem. The account, as in any mythical story, has many possible applications and dimensions of meaning and lends itself to a variety of interpretations.

Thus we must speak of primary and secondary applications. I am convinced that the primary import of the original story impinges directly on what we today call the possibility and limitation of human technology, and that the insight of the prophets who wrote the biblical account is profoundly realistic. A careful analysis of the symbolism and literary structure will reveal this.

The story is about the original husband and wife who are at home in the "garden"—the fruitful earth—that God has created for them. Everything has been provided for their sustenance and welfare. They are living in harmony with the other animals God had created. They have domesticated some animals and some remain untamed, but not a threat. All the plants have been given to them for food, but God warned them that the fruit of one tree is poisonous. It will cause death. That tree is called "the tree of the knowledge of good and evil." A serpent, one of the "wild animals" (Gen. 3:1), challenges God's warning. (Did Eve see the serpent in the tree eating the fruit without suffering dire affects?) It claims that the taboo forbidding them to eat the fruit is the result of divine jealousy. The wife is the one the serpent approaches. Apparently up to this time she had not given much attention to the fruit, and when she examined it she discovered that it was good for food. Taking one bite out of the fruit did not kill her! So she gave it to Adam to sample.

But clearly this is not the end of the story. Although they did not drop dead, their disobedience displeased God, who moved immediately to deny them access to the "tree of life" which was also planted in the garden. They lost their relation of trusting dependence on God, and they found their resultant lives full of sweat and anxiety! Their special likeness and relation to God, described as being created in "God's image" (1:26), gave them the authority as God's regents to "subdue the earth" (1:28), but their disobedience affected their relation to the environing earth. Adam's work became laborious and frustrating. The results of his agricultural efforts (primitive technology) were uncertain and grudging. Eve found herself subservient to her partner, cursed with the pain of childbearing and menial status. And when Adam begot a son it was "in his own image," not God's (5:1-3)—that is, birth of a new generation was not a "new beginning" that recovered the original condition. The malfunction and frustration continue!

The Nature of Technology

To understand the biblical perspective on technology, we must first understand the essential nature of technology. With this background we can then examine the symbolism of the Genesis account.

The word *technology* comes from the root word *techni*[*que*] (art or craft) plus *logos*—a reasoned invention of effective technique for accomplishing human goals. It presupposes a specialized knowledge and skill, and its purpose is practical. In science we differentiate between the theoretical and technical/practical sciences. Engineering, for example, is a technical science. Technical colleges train students for doing things, not for philosophizing or doing "pure research." However, the dividing line between the two blurs, and it is arguable that there really is little or no moral difference.

Some think of technology as a kind of mechanical tool such as a wrench or hammer. Or, to change the comparison, as a mathematical formula which describes and opens up the world around us for our modification and use. It is assumed to be a rational (in contrast to magical) means which contributes to human welfare. As such it is considered an unambiguous good, a morally neutral means which can be used either for good or evil. The problematic involved in its pursuit simply has to do with its use.

But technology is more than a simple mechanical technique. It is a branch of science that applies the theoretical knowledge of empirical research to the wants and needs of the human family. It is part of a human system of knowledge with its own view of human existence, its own presuppositions, jargon, and methodology. Its goal is to bring the world of nature under human control ("subdue"). It depends on precise empirical analysis, human imagination, and craft. Its methodology has no place for magic or God—that is, for an unexplained or uncontrollable power outside its own realm of operations. As I write, for example, there is a debate in the medical profession about the effectiveness of prayer in the healing process, between what we might call the medical technocrats and those who admit the value of a spiritual intervention. But even in this case the evidence for the effectiveness of prayer tends to turn it into a technique which can be managed.

The human temptation is to make technology a self-sufficient, self-regulating discipline, and in a moment of hubris to think that nothing is impossible—"the difficult today and the impossible tomorrow." According to this logic, there are no limits to human knowledge, and technology is the way to gain knowledge. Therefore, if it *can* be done, it *should* be done.

The goal of technology is the human *manipulation* and *control* of the environment to human advantage. In contrast to magic, which also aims at human manipulation and control of human environment and destiny, technology, as said above, is a reasoned human process. The technological approach considers the environing physical universe an impersonal "thing," something detached from the technician him/herself. It desacralizes and depersonalizes the natural environment for the purpose of objective research and manipulation. For example, the human body is considered a machine as exploration of the brain, birth control, genetic engineering, cloning, and implanting of nanocomputer chips into the human physical system unfold. Although ancient technology had not reached the levels of our Western world, its essential nature has not changed. The technology of the ancient world was surprisingly sophisticated, as archeological research is constantly showing us

Biblical Ambivalence About Technology

In the Bible technology plays an ambiguous role. It is both implied in the mandate to the human pair to "subdue the earth," and it is the point at which humanity's self-awareness of its limitation is tested. The second-century theologian and martyr, Irenaeus, understood this well. He interpreted Adam and Eve's innocence not as perfection far superior to ours, which they lost, but as child-likeness, which had the potential for growth into the true image of God as portrayed in Christ, the "Son of God."[1] The image of God was their destiny, and the responsible management of "the garden," through what we now refer to as technology, was their mandate. Thus it is precisely the moral limits of their management of technology that is at question when the serpent talks to Eve.

The desirability and necessity of technology is implied already in the Creator's mandate to the human family to "have dominion" over the animal world and to "subdue" the earth (Gen. 1:28). And in the second account of the creation, the original human pair were commanded to "till and keep" the garden (2:15), a command which clearly implies at least an agricultural technology. The ambivalence seems to arise when technology has advanced to the point of building cities (Babel/ Babylon). Problematic advancement of technology is in the first place associated with the descendents of Cain who, the account says, built cities and developed metallurgy (4:17, 22).

The story of the building of the city of Babylon, sometimes referred to as the second story of the Fall, points clearly to the problem. While there is no proscription on gathering together and building cities, Babylon becomes the symbol of the human city in contrast to the New Jerusalem, the heavenly city. Its origins are in the proud attempt of the people in the plains of Shinar to build themselves a city and in it a tower to heaven (11:4). Archaeologists identify this tower with the ziggurat, temple of Marduk, the god of Babylon. The "tower with its top in the heavens," which is described as the product of the advanced technology of brick making and building (v. 3), was likely a symbol of the sacred axis between heaven and earth. As such it represented a place of power where the devotees could manipulate heaven for their own use. When the Lord God saw what mortals were doing, he said, "Look, they are one people, and they have all one language; and this is only the beginning of what they will do; nothing that they propose to do will now be impossible for them" (11:7). Here technology is associated with the idolatrous attempt to manage and control one's own human destiny, and God scatters the population ostensibly to hinder such human endeavors.

This prophetic assessment of the ambivalence of technology comes as no surprise when we read it in light of the story of the primal temptation of the first human pair. In that story already the teaser lies in deciphering the goods and evils of life. Its meaning lies in the symbolism of its characters. There is first of all the "tree of the knowledge of good and evil," with God's warning. Then enters the serpent that accosts the woman. We need to understand each of these to understand the significance of this prophetic warning against arrogant self-reliance and the danger of relying on human technology to achieve the true goods of life.

Tree of knowledge of good and evil

The knowledge associated with "the tree in the middle of the garden" has from the earliest centuries been interpreted as sexual knowledge. Clement of Alexandria (d. ca 212 A.D.) taught that Adam and Eve were childlike and innocent, and God planned for them to grow up stage by stage. Sexual knowledge was not evil in itself as some Gnostics taught, but it was to be delayed until they were properly developed. "The fault of Adam and Eve consisted in the fact that, using their volition wrongly, they indulged in the pleasures of sexual intercourse before God gave them leave."[2] For this reason they lost the gift of immortal life.

This is not the place to trace the centuries of debate about the nature of the knowledge that was poisonous. It will suffice to say that it was generally assumed that originally Adam was a perfectly rational being far superior to humans as we now know ourselves, who as a result of his disobedience became morally guilty (lost his innocence) and subject to death. The consequences of his "fall from original righteousness," according to Augustine, was a bent to self-indulgence epitomized by sexual lust (concupiscence) and loss of the freedom not to sin.[3]

This conception of knowledge reflects the cultural prejudices of the age, which inflated the significance of physical sexual experience and overrated the virtue of asceticism. We need first to understand that there is nothing in the Hebrew words "good and evil" that particularly suggest moral right and wrong. The word for knowledge derives from *yada*, the general word for knowledge (including sexual knowledge), and suggests cunning, cleverness, or becoming aware. The words for good and evil denote good in the widest sense—human welfare, well-being, beauty, and evil as adversity, affliction, mischief, misery, and badness—"everything good and evil." So we must conclude that while this knowledge may include the growing awareness of right and wrong, it by no means is limited to sexual experience. Neither is there any reason to think that the dawning of moral awareness itself is the primary meaning. The guilty reactions of Adam and Eve as depicted in the story indicate the breaking of a primitive taboo rather than a clear moral awareness of ethical infraction.

The serpent offered Eve knowledge of how to succeed in her role as Adam's "helper" by her own clever know-how—a knowledge that would give her the ability to more effectively control her life and augment their livelihood. He suggests that it will give her power and take the insecurity and dependence factors out of life. "You can be like the gods!" And, he adds, God knew this, and that is why he denied its fruit to you. This is the kind of practical knowledge that we call technical—the subject of technology.

"The Woman"[4]

Many reasons have been offered for why the serpent approached the woman. Most if not all of them take the anthropological bias of the first century and Paul as their basic interpretive cue, namely that women are the weaker sex both intellectually and morally (2 Cor. 11:3) and are to be subservient to their husbands. By implication, the observation in 1 Timothy 2:13-14 that "Adam was formed first, then Eve; *and Adam was not deceived, but the woman was deceived and became a transgressor*" (emph. added) provided the rationale for the serpent's approach to the woman. At best some commentators partly excused Eve by noting that it was Adam who heard the command directly from God and she only had it on the word of her husband.

Traditional theology assumed that moral weakness and vulnerability of the woman was the hermeneutical key to the serpent's approach. Some commentators have even suggested that after her own disobedience, Eve used her sexual wiles to persuade Adam to eat of the fruit! But a careful reading of the narrative suggests another more cogent reason.

Eve was Adam's *wife*, and the wife was the manager of the household upon whom the daily tasks of food preparation and homemaking fell. Anthropologists note that in agrarian peasant societies women have control over resources and decisions. As Susan Carol Rogers argues, "although peasant males monopolize positions of authority and are shown public deference by women, thus superficially appearing to be dominant, they wield relatively little real power. . . [W]ithin the context of peasant society, women control at least the major portion of important resources and decisions."[5] Thus when Eve saw that the fruit "was good for food" (it didn't kill the snake), that it had real decorative possibilities ("a delight to the eye"), and would improve her skills and enhance her livelihood ("would make her wise/clever"), she was interested in the serpent's claim. This is the language of everyday technology—and brings us to the role of the serpent.

The serpent

Again, in traditional theologies the serpent is simply assumed to be the devil in all of his malevolent cunning, as described in later Christian mythology, bent on destroying God's handiwork. The temptation is presented in stark either-or terms of good and evil. Adam and Eve before the "Fall" are assumed to be creatures of pristine perfection morally, intellectually, and spiritually. Thus when Eve is tempted to doubt God's goodness and intentions for their welfare, yielding to the temptation is an act of unconscionable rebellion which can be accounted for only by her weakness as a female. And according to 1 Timothy, Adam was tricked into eating the tabooed fruit in such a way that he did not share the full moral weight of the infraction. "*Adam was not deceived*, but the woman was deceived and became a transgressor" (v. 13, emph. added). The result is morally guilty creatures who have "fallen" from their "original righteousness," and in whom the "image of God" is corrupted.

While this is not an impossible reading of the story, it fails to recognize the nature and ambiguity of the temptation and the resultant human situation. In the ancient world the serpent was a symbol of both beneficial and harmful powers that humankind has to deal with. The account refers to it as one of the creatures that had not been domesticated and calls it "more crafty than any other creature" (3:1). In Egypt the serpent was a divinity of fertility—probably its origin as a medical symbol. Also the spreading cobra head was a symbol on the Pharaoh's crown, which suggests a symbol of authority and power.

Among Canaanites the serpent was worshipped as a goddess who could cause both harm and blessing. In Matthew 10:16 the phrase "wise as serpents" might more properly be translated "clever [*phronimos*] as serpents." Thus clearly the serpent does not symbolize a sinister, immoral creature, but precisely one that fits with our categories of pragmatic, practical, clever, ambiguous, looking out for oneself. It subtly twists God's warning and suggests that God is afraid that they will join the divinities that compete with divine power.

Naked humans

The account seems to make a special point out of the humans' nakedness, which I understand to be their vulnerability. Adam and Eve were vulnerable and naive, "innocent" in the sense of inexperienced. They were living in the "Garden of Eden"—a symbol for the fruitful earth, which God had created to sustain and nourish the human family. Theirs is a simple, idyllic agricultural existence, living in harmony with nature, eating vegetables that God had given to both them and the other animals for food. In such an original condition they were unaware of their "nakedness."

In this setting the serpent promises, "I can give you the kind of knowledge that will allow you to control and 'develop' your primitive existence." In Hebrew the words *naked* and *crafty* form a kind of pun, suggesting that humans lacked what the serpent had. Technical know-how could expand and enhance their primitive existence. They would not be at the whim of God (Nature?) to supply their everyday needs. By implication the knowledge offered them by the serpent represented a managerial possibility for controlling and fulfilling life's meaning—the achievement of the "image of God"—by their own inventive skill. The temptation was to take control of their lives beyond and in disregard of the limitation the Creator had placed on them. The kind of practical knowledge the serpent offered was not wrong in itself. Indeed, as we have seen, God's mandate implied the need for such knowledge, but the serpent represented technological knowledge and skill to achieve the true end of life apart from dependence on the Creator.

"You will surely die!"

The temptation was to use power selfishly, and as God had warned, it turned out that such power is the power of death. The "technological fix" is self-defeating. When humans overstep their bounds, when they "play God" they merely raise the ante, or in biblical language, they lose their innocence. In the technological solution lies an unspoken but ineradicable contradiction—a *surd* (a number or quantity that cannot be expressed as the ratio of two integers) if you please. While technical solutions may seem to be an immediate advantage—to Eve it looked good and clever—they invariably also exacerbate the problems and demand new technological interventions. Karl Marx was certainly correct when he observed that at some point *quantitative* (technological) change creates *qualitative* difference. The biblical view is that there is no technological fix for the ultimate problem of humanity, which is "death."

In our postmodern world we have begun to lose confidence in the unmitigated benefit of technology. There is a growing recognition of its built-in ambiguity. Often its immediate beneficial results carry within them the seeds of future harmful consequences. These ill effects are not only the results of mistakes in technology: They point to the dilemma built into the technological process itself. Deleterious effects in an ascending spiral that in turn must be addressed inescapably accompany every advance. Technology is not an unambiguous, unqualified, self-regulating good that can and will ultimately solve the world's problems. It is a *human* process, which needs to be controlled by a transcending rational-moral purpose or, in biblical theological terms, by God.

In the Genesis story, when the Creator saw that humans were set on their own way, he removed the possibility of eating the fruit of the *tree of life*. Understood in this way, the story of the primal temptation and sin raises the true nature of the question that faces us. What are the moral limits to technological control and how are they to be enforced? The rest of the biblical story addresses the human problem in these terms and offers God's continuing alternative.

Notes

1. See Justo Gonzalez, *A History of Christian Thought*, rev. ed., vol. 1 (Nashville: Abingdon, 1980),161-62.
2. J. N. D. Kelly, *Early Christian Doctrines* (New York: Harper Brothers, 1958), 179.
3. Ibid., 361-66.
4. For a historical account of the convoluted explanations of Gnostic and Orthodox theologians of the woman's role in the temptation story see Elaine Pagels, *Adam, Eve, and the Serpent* (New York: Random House, 1988).
5. Quoted by John Dominic Crossan in "Jesus and the Kingdom," in *Jesus at 2000*, ed. Marcus Borg (Boulder, Co: Westview Press, 1998), 25. This certainly was the case in traditional Japanese society, where even into the modern urban setting the wife has major control of the family's life and resources even though she does not share equal dignity. It has been quite customary for the husband to hand over his salary to the wife and receive back his spending allowance for the week.

10

The Beginning of the Assembly Congregation: A Theological Reflection

I remember clearly, although I'm not sure why, a statement I first made one Sunday morning in a sermon to the Maple Grove Mennonite congregation in Topeka, Indiana in the early 1950s. I said, "The most important things going on in the world at this time are not happening in Washington, D.C., Moscow, or London. They are happening amid the local communities of believers." I think that ideal of the local congregation still characterized our basic conviction in the late 1960s and early 1970s when some of us requested that the College Mennonite Church grant us the privilege of experimenting under its auspices with more participatory forms of the local congregation. After some two decades of serving in the institutional church programs, we were not persuaded that the more formal and perfunctory approaches to church were effectively representing the kingdom of God.

Those of us promoting intensive small groups as the basic organic unit of the congregation were not alone in this frustration with local congregational life. In a lecture to a Humane Studies Program Workshop in spring 1974, professor Daniel Hess opined that the congregation must give us a vantage point from which the Humane Studies Program could proceed, and he decried the congregational situation in many of our Mennonite churches in terms with which many of us agreed. He said, in part,

> An even larger question pertains to the current state of many congregations. I am not referring here to the rather superficial

> annoyances such as not liking the preacher or being dissatisfied with the meeting time. Instead, there seems to be a widespread failing of congregational health. Mennonites have not found effective congregational forms for its [sic] post-1960 membership. Where the church has borrowed from other major American denominations and dioceses, the results have compromised the commitment.
>
> Congregations know they are in trouble and deserve criticism. But the servant to whom they might turn for help has not delivered the imaginative help he ought to give.

The Assembly vision grew out of this troubling realization that something was missing in our church congregational life. During the first half of the twentieth century, the Mennonite church had given highest priority to the development of a denominational structure—institutional boards and programs such as missions, publications, and education. Congregations were continuing old patterns of organization and worship, or where changing, they were adopting traditional protestant patterns with little attempt to adjust them to reflect the values of Anabaptist-Mennonite community life.

The 1960s and early 1970s were a dynamic period of turmoil, protest, and experimentation. The nonviolent protests of the civil rights movement were still active, and Vietnam War protests were in high gear. Vatican II still provided excitement on the ecumenical front. Therapy groups were emphasizing face-to-face, uninhibited expression as the way to personal and social health. The charismatic movement was at its height. Church leadership seminars and retreats were stressing egalitarianism and the importance of the "gifts of the Spirit" among all the people of God (laity). Koinonia Farm, the Society of Brothers, the Reba Place Fellowship, and Church of the Savior, to mention only a few independent church groups, provided precedents and challenges.

In all this social and political turbulence, many Mennonite college students were deciding that the church was not a significant broker for change. Of those who were still attending Sunday morning services many were seeking out congregations where more spontaneous emotional expression was encouraged.

In the early 1970s, the Goshen College Church congregation experienced a significant decline in student attendance, and those of us who were directly involved with student life felt that the congregation was not responding adequately to the new challenges. This in brief was the context in which we began what came to be known for lack of a formal name as the Assembly Mennonite Church.

Ecclesiological Focus

Theologically considered, our concerns were mainly the identity and mission of the church. We strongly affirmed the lordship of Jesus Christ as presented in the New Testament, and we understood salvation as life in a new order of relationships under his authority. We understood that the local congregations of the church were to be the saved and saving communities expressing the new order of the kingdom in which individuals found meaning and purpose for their lives "in Christ." We understood this phrase, "in Christ," to mean more than a mystical or spiritual relation to Christ. It included being in the "body of Christ."

In our earliest covenant confession we simply confessed Jesus as Lord, not "Savior and Lord," to underscore this corporate sense of salvation. Christ was our Savior by virtue of being Lord and "head of the church." As head of the body he both nourished and directed the church, enabling it to become "the body of Christ." The words *Savior and* were added several years later when some felt that we should be more explicit in our confession of Christ as Savior.

We were clearly focused on the New Testament, but we used it as a model for our church life, not so much for a theological textbook of doctrines. For us the new life in Christ, both in its individual and social aspects, was the focus, not so much a correct system of doctrine. I think it would be unfair to say that we were "hung up" on the Sermon on the Mount, but we certainly did not read the letters of Paul from a Lutheran perspective in contrast to the Gospels! Rather Paul's emphasis on participation (*koinonia*) in Christ—in his life and mission, and his call to a new social expression of life in Christ—motivated us.

Potential members were not required to be firmly committed to certain doctrinal formulas or practical applications (not even on the peace issues); rather, they covenanted to sincerely engage with us in the study of Scripture and pledge to follow the leading of the Spirit through the congregation. From the beginning, denominational lines ceased to have meaning for us, although we never discussed the issue as such. To "belong" meant simply to actively participate in the congregational life. As soon as we formed an independent congregation, we applied for dual membership in both the Mennonite Church and General Conference Mennonite denominational conferences of that era.

Participation in congregational life meant far more to us than attendance at Sunday morning group worship. Our Sunday "assembly" was the congregating of small groups, which we called "K groups" (K for koinonia); membership included belonging to one of these groups. That, in fact, was how we got our name, "Assembly." We were an assembly of small ecclesial groups. One joined the Assembly by becoming a member of a small group which in turn sponsored the individual for assembly membership. When people were drawn to our Sunday morning services, we encouraged them to take this route to full membership.

These K groups, or house churches, were the centers of accountability and discernment. The group studied Scripture. It counseled and prayed together. Pastoral care began here in the face-to-face weekly meeting. Issues facing the larger group were carefully discussed in an attempt to arrive at small-group consensus. In this way Assembly business was first processed and representatives from the groups reported discussion and discernment to the larger assembly. Our deliberate choice of terms like *representatives* and *coordinators* for our congregational leaders underscored the seriousness with which we took our egalitarian organization.

Exclusive or Inclusive Community?

We were keenly aware of the dangers and baneful effects of schism and splintering, and we were self-consciously aware of the potential for intensive small groups to splinter. While our protest inevitably implied criticism of traditional Protestant church patterns, our intent was not so much to withdraw and be a perfect congregation as to find ways in which we along with the wider church could more authentically confirm the life and ethic of the kingdom of God among us.

To this end we asked the College congregation, of which many of us were members, to commission us as a working experiment to explore new possible patterns of congregational life. And as soon as we were organized as an independent congregation, to our surprise and delight leaders of the Indiana-Michigan Conference invited us to formally join the conference in such a capacity. We chose Mary Ellen Meyer as our first congregational representative to conference.

An almost reflexive impulse to splinter was inherent in our protest, and as I look back I am amazed and grateful for the patience shown on both sides. A number of the small groups that eventually consolidated to form the Assembly had originally formed out of disillusionment with the existing organizations and in protest to them. These groups thought of their life together as a substitute for the institutional church—a kind of "true church." Indeed, some of these groups quite openly thought of themselves as a prophetic witness to the church—a stance not greatly appreciated by the main body. They recognized their own leaders as prophetic authorities, and they held their own services of Bible study and worship.

Further, tendencies to exclusivism developed within some small groups as a result of intensive communal sharing. There was strong emphasis on personal disclosure and trust that required intimate exposure of oneself. Such relationships, considered the hallmark of the true church, could only be developed over time and demanded strict confidentiality. This raised the difficulty both of inducting new members into the group and of joining with other groups of similar character. It was in the context of these strains and stresses that the Assembly congregation was born, and we struggled to become a community of the Spirit at once committed to spiritual fervor and intimacy and at the same time open and accepting of any who might be attracted to us.

This attempt at what I may call evangelical openness involved us in a self-conscious attempt to avoid legalism and moralism. We wanted to allow those who were questing and questioning (doubting) the freedom to do so within the bounds of covenant. Indeed, we understood, as Paul Tillich had pointed out, that doubt is not to be equated with unbelief. Rather it is a vital aspect of faith. Thus we drew up a covenant of membership in terms of loyalty and the pledge to be faithful to the way of Jesus as it became manifest. The covenant affirmed recognition of Christ's lordship, a pledge of responsibility to each other as God's people, and commitment to help each other find and faithfully obey Christ's mandate.

We distinguished between this kind of pledge and what we called "understandings." The understandings spelled out the consensus which the congregation of small groups had arrived at thus far in its ongoing discussion. These understandings described clearly the perspectives and accumulated agreements of our group so that anyone interested in membership would have to take them seriously, but at the same time they were open to the continuing discernment of the group in light of new perspectives brought to it by the new person.

The first listing of these understandings, interestingly enough, did not include a statement of our peace convictions. We concentrated on the nature of the group relationships and necessary commitments to group participation, such as full attendance at small and large group meetings, willingness to receive counsel, maintaining a loving open spirit toward those who were exploring our group life, and a commitment to faithful stewardship. This did not indicate that there was any softness on the peace position. Rather, certain immediate concerns took precedence in the process of formation. Once these procedural matters were firmly in position, further ongoing issues could be considered. We took a clear, and some would say, radical position on the importance and implications of peacemaking "in all areas of life."

Church as Sacrament

We were fully convinced that the church itself as the body of Christ was to be the sacramental presence of Christ in the world. In the words of John's Gospel, congregations are branches sustained and nourished by the vine, and as such are part of the vine bearing fruit in the world. This defines both the congregation's life and mission.

The church does not find its sacramental reality in a ceremony, but rather celebrates its sacramental reality in ceremonial forms. The sacramental significance of the ceremony is determined by the reality of the Spirit in the everyday life of the congregation. That is why Paul warned the Corinthian Christians to be careful of the manner in which they proceeded to the communion table (1 Cor. 11:27-32). The problem was not the profaning of a sacred ceremony but of misrepresenting the true nature of Christ's sacramental presence in the world.

The congregation embodies the Spirit of Christ in its *koinoniac* existence. Such koinoniac existence locates the sacramental nature of the church in the character of its personal-social life in the world, i.e., in its koinoniac character. This means first, participation in Christ who is "head of the church" and nourishes and nurtures its life together in the world (the spiritual reality). It also indicates participation of individuals in the community of believers (the social reality). Individuals share in and become part of the sacramental reality of Christ as they participate in the "fellowship of the Spirit." Thus the sacramental character of the church engages it in both the saving life and mission of Christ.

We attempted to portray this understanding of the nature of the church in our celebration of baptism and the Lord's Supper. Our earliest baptismal service, held in the old College Cabin, engaged the congregation and the applicants in a liturgy of shared confession. The congregation first addressed the applicants: "We have pledged to renounce our sin of selfish ambition and to bind ourselves under the authority of Jesus Christ to live in his body and holy community, the church, according to his rule and kingdom." The applicants were then asked to respond with a like pledge. Thereafter the congregation affirmed its confession of faith, and the applicants were asked whether they shared this faith and would pledge loyalty to Jesus Christ. Upon this confession they were baptized as a sign of God's pledge to forgive and accept them into the family of God and received as members of "the community of Christ's Holy Spirit."

I should pause to highlight the content of our confession of faith, since it was not a traditional doctrinal statement. Our confession focused on God's action on our behalf through "His son, Jesus of Nazareth," and the nature of our response. (We were not yet so politically correct that we always had to avoid the masculine pronoun when speaking of God.) We confessed that in Jesus God had come to us in our likeness, suffering the bitterness of our rejection and the stigma of our sin to reconcile us, and had demonstrated divine power over sin and death by raising Jesus from the dead. We affirmed our confidence in the new possibility of life and freedom through the gift of the Spirit, and we committed ourselves to live in the hope that God will fully establish the kingdom of peace and justice with Jesus Christ as Lord of lords and King of kings.

While the confession implied a high Christology, it did not spell this out in terms of orthodoxy's philosophical dualism. The confession located the fundamental response as an existential commitment to Jesus, "the true and living way" rather than belief in the paradox of his deity and humanity. It affirmed hope and the new possibility of life in the Spirit as motivation for the Christian life, in contrast to relief from guilt feelings and the fear of punishment. In this manner we attempted to define an experiential basis for a discipleship that was more than ethical response to theological belief. The motivation for following Christ lay in our conviction that he truly is God's Savior, and his Spirit in and through us creates the dynamic possibility.

In our celebration of the Lord's Supper, we emphasized the eucharistic element. Our "communion" was a celebration of the new covenant given in Christ, a thanksgiving for the spiritual food which we received at the Lord's table. As such it implied the catholicity, i.e., unity, of the body of Christ. It was not so much a celebration of our exclusive existence as of our sharing in the universal reality of his body. We did not stress the renewal of our loyalty pledge so much as Christ's gift of himself to us. The blood was a symbol of Jesus' life given for us. The bread was a symbol of Christ's sharing of himself in and through the congregation. We shared the bread and cup with each other as an indication that we belonged to one family of God, and as a pledge of respect and family responsibility for each other.

The Congregation's Mission

One of our central, pervading concerns was to preserve the unity of life together in the congregation and the mission of the congregation in the larger society. We were not motivated by perfectionistic or sectarian goals. We sought to be a community of the Spirit amid, not apart from, the larger society. In *The Community of the Spirit,* which I was writing at that time, I spoke of the church in this sense as a *secular* community, i.e., a very real aspect of the larger social phenomenon. In an early report from the Mission Task Force to the congregation, I defined the mission of the congregation to be the propagation of itself as a dynamic community of the Holy Spirit under the covenant of Jesus Christ. It was to be a social catalyst for the continual emergence of the power and authority of God in creating community. Today this is commonly spoken of as being an anticipatory community of the kingdom of God.

To that end we recognized humanitarian service, evangelism, and education as simply complementary components of the one mission. Although we recognized their distinctive functions, it was impossible to sharply divide and contrast their objectives. In the same report mentioned above, I warned against the temptation of letting each of these roles become ends in themselves. Their common goal, I said, is the "new creation," the "new humanity," reconciliation and life in God's family under the new covenant. I pointed out that humanitarian service as an end had very largely resulted in creating dependency and consumerism. Evangelism as an end had largely resulted in individualistic religious experience which had little effect in advancing the new humanity. And education as an end had largely perpetuated the tradition, adjusting and adapting it to the changing social climate. What was needed was a witness which in itself demonstrated the power of the Spirit to keep a chain reaction going.

It was this theological motivation along with other practical concerns that led us to consider finding an off-campus site for our meetings. While we all agreed that students were an important focus of our mission, some of us were afraid that meeting on campus identified us too closely with institutionalized education. And since by this time we were large enough to require division, after much deliberation we decided to meet in two locations—one off and one on campus. Our off-campus "cluster" wrestled with the practicality and significance of a place that would give us a presence and identity in the city. For a while we used an empty dance hall and a funeral parlor for cluster meetings and the city park for "sabbatical" assembly meetings. Finally we located an old sewing factory on Eleventh Street which could be remodeled and used for both types of meetings as well as a center for community witness. It took us several years to discover how we could be more effective in reaching a totally unchurched population. (That is a story in itself.)

Worship in the Life of the Congregation

Lest anyone think that our congregational life was one of endless academic discussions about the nature of the church and constant business meetings, let me hasten to add that our community came to a full crescendo of praise and fellowship in the Sunday morning worship service."It was then that we celebrated who we were in the service of God, and it was a joyous time of heartfelt expression.

We observed that the New Testament word *leiturgeo*, usually translated worship, meant priestly service. In the Jewish tradition such service was usually associated with the temple celebrations as the priests ministered in behalf of the people. Their *leiturgia* (service) to God was expressed in their service to and for the congregation as they ministered in the temple. We as the new people of God and living stones in God's temple were simply adopting and expanding this concept of worship as we performed our priestly service to God with and for each other. I remember thinking and saying on occasion that the phrase *worship service* was really redundant! Our service of God with and for the community of God's people was our "worship," and the celebration on Sunday morning was simply part of that larger life of worship.

We were an assembly of "priests" meeting in God's presence to offer our service in honor of God's goodness and authority among us, i.e. to "hallow God's name." It was our purpose to more fully understand and do God's will "on earth as it is in heaven." In this sense we understood worship as an act of kingdom business, and we explicitly said that our congregational business meetings were no less worship than Sunday morning services of praise and exhortation.

This emphasis on leiturgia led us to stress the need for congruence of form and content in the service. In trying to explain this concern, I once spoke of liturgy as the "complimentary choreography" of meaning and action. We spent a great deal of time and energy on the development of liturgy; however, we tried to move away from liturgy as ceremonial programming. We were attempting to find effective patterns for genuine participation in the service. Thus we focused on functions in the service—singing/dancing, reading Scripture, preaching/teaching, giving, praying, testifying, and not to be omitted, silence. How does one choreograph this sequence so that the whole congregation is caught up in the leiturgia?

While our services on Sunday morning were inspirational and deeply satisfying, the subjective inspiration of individuals was not our focus. Rather, our focus was upon what God was doing in our lives as individuals and a congregation as well as in the world. Our worship was our response to God's initiative. As Professor Paul Lehman at Princeton Theological Seminary used to put it, we were "trying to discover what God was doing in the world and then get on his bandwagon." We hoped for two outcomes of our worship: first, to discover our true identity as God's people, and second, to find enablement for authentic discipleship. We viewed reverence not as a pious mood but as obedient action!

Perhaps this observation is a good note upon which to close. Obedient action and authenticity were our watchwords. We took them very seriously. Indeed, sometimes we undoubtedly took ourselves too seriously. But in all our intensity we also had a theology of play! In our Metanonia group we rather unpiously (not impiously) adapted the slogan, "The family that prays together stays together" to fit our group life and experience. We said, "The family that plays together stays together." We found this to be literally true. Intense as they were, I remember even our worship times as re-creational play!

11

How My Mind Has Changed

I was raised in a milieu of strict literal biblicism. The King James Version of the Bible said what it meant and meant what it said! If one compared the authority of the Bible with that of the *Encyclopedia Britannica,* as might happen in high school, the encyclopedia did not have a chance. A vague evolutionary perspective was presented in science classes, but the issue was not pushed. It had not been that many years since the Scopes trial in Tennessee, and public high school teachers in Virginia did not risk offending the faithful. The most that might be conceded by our church leaders was that the six days of creation may have been longer periods of time, but even that compromise with literal meaning raised suspicions of liberalism.

In the church community, Bishop George R. Brunk, who had adopted the premillennialist prophetic hermeneutic as the most literal, common-sense interpretation of Scripture, was the scholarly authority. To this day I can almost reproduce from memory the premillennial prophetic chart, designed by J. B. Smith, which "G. R. B." used. His *Ready Scriptural Reasons*, *Rightly Dividing the Scriptures*, and his quarterly periodical, the *Sword and Trumpet,* in which he tried to outdo the Fundamentalists at their own game, provided my early theological fare.

The standard definitions of *inspiration* and *revelation*, which we were taught in college Bible classes, were worded in such a way as to avoid the concept of dictation while at the same time affirming a divinely controlled process of communication that produced an error-free text in the original biblical documents. The basic work of the Holy Spirit in the past was the "inspiration" of Scripture, and in the present it is the illumination of the spiritual mind to properly understand that inspired text. One did not expect any new "revelation," since that was equated with the inspired biblical text, but only the illumination of the text.

This template was still firmly in place well into the 1950s in our Mennonite church colleges, when I began to teach in the Bible department at Goshen College. Indeed it was not formally revised in the (Old) Mennonite circles until the 1963 *Confession of Faith,* although certain aspects of the theory had been under discussion and modification for at least the previous decade.

I have begun with this background because it provides the backdrop for crucial changes in my own thinking. I should point out at the beginning that the issue for me was not so much the *authority* of Scripture as the *semantic nature* of its text. Semantics relates to the meaning and use of language. But of course differences in one's semantic point of view affect the nature and application of its authority.

It became clear to me in my study of the early church that even Christian leaders of late antiquity did not base biblical authority on an inerrant text. In fact, Origen (ca. 185-254 A. D.) used the errors that he perceived at the literal historical level to demonstrate the necessity for an allegorical, or spiritual, interpretation of Scripture. Further, I came to understand that the very nature of the communication process makes language a questionable tool for an inerrant transmission of ideas. *Meaning* depends on both the speaker/writer and the hearer/reader. Thus over centuries of time historical changes in context are bound to affect the meaning of scriptural texts. There is no way in which a "literal" text could preserve an inerrant original meaning as the reading and interpretation of the Bible crosses centuries and cultures.

Of course this did not come as an immediate revelation. My special interest in graduate school was Christian thought, and as I studied the historical development of Christian theology I came to see the significance of the concept of *historical* revelation in contrast, for example, to the Islamic *oracular* concept. *God's revelation came as a self-disclosure of divine nature, presence, and activity in Yahweh's interaction with Israel culminating in Jesus as the Messiah.* Thus Jesus stands as the climax and norm for revelation, not the Bible. And Jesus left his Holy Spirit to continue his own revelatory mission, not the Bible. The Bible is the record and witness to this self-revealing interaction up through the coming of

Jesus and the establishing of an apostolic witness. Although we know the Jesus of history through the historical record, we come to know Jesus as the authentic Word of God through the work of the Spirit. Thus we must learn to read the Bible in the light of the Spirit's continuing disclosure of Jesus and not vice versa.

This in turn led me to a different understanding of the work of the Holy Spirit in the production and use of Scripture. The Spirit "inspires" both the recording and the authentic understanding of what is written. The Spirit enabled (inspired) the original disciples to recognize the significance of the crucified and resurrected Jesus. This same Spirit inspires the authentic contextualization of the biblical message as it is translated across cultures. Thus we may speak of the Bible as "Holy Spirit inspired" when it is understood and used to authentically promote the Spirit of Jesus.

The Holy Spirit does not produce an inspired text that henceforth will be the revelation for God's people. As the "executive of revelation," to use a phrase from B. B. Warfield, the Spirit *is* God's self-disclosing presence with God's people. (This is not, of course, to imply that the Spirit is not universally present and active as creative sustainer in the universe.) The Spirit is in fact the Reality in which "we live and move and have our being" as Paul put it in Acts 18, and "revelation" is this ongoing self-disclosing, interactive Presence making itself known in historical personal-social relationship. It should not be equated with an inspired written text.

This new understanding of the dynamic relation of Spirit and word freed me to read the Bible from varying cultural perspectives as I taught in the Asian context. I required a new criterion for evaluating contemporary interpretations of Scripture. The old norm was "orthodoxy," namely, faithfulness to the great Western tradition of the church. The new norm was "authenticity," namely, faithfulness to the Spirit of Christ. Of course, the tradition of the church dare not be lightly dismissed, but it is not the final authority! For example, the orthodox concept of "Trinity" needs to be taken seriously, but not as a procrustean bed into which all theological statements about God, Jesus, and the Spirit must arbitrarily fit.

A second area of change in my theological outlook relates to the church as a social community. What does it mean from a sociological perspective to be the "body of Christ," a "colony of heaven," or "salt of the earth" amid a secular society?

I was raised in a Mennonite "colony" that was a self-sustaining community of Pennsylvania Dutch Mennonites who had migrated to southern Virginia at the end of the nineteenth century. Tidewater Virginia was an English, post-plantation society and economy, and the "Dutch" group functioned as a sectarian socioeconomic community within it. The church house and farm home of the bishop were literally and symbolically at its geographic center. In the 1940s, when the church was exploring anew what it meant to be "in the world but not of the world," it became one sociological type for the Mennonite Community movement.

My changing perspective here was from a sectarian-denominational model of church community, not to institutional ecumenism, but to a *grassroots ecumenism.* I was and am convinced that a "kingdom" model of church requires a grassroots pattern of ecumenical fellowship after the model of the Church of the Savior, communities like Clarence Jordan's Koinonia Farm in Georgia, and the Sojourners community in Washington, D. C. It was with such a pattern in mind that I wrote *The Community of the Spirit* and *The Authentic Witness.*

Today I tend to view the church as a community of the Spirit and define its unity as sharing a common concern, purpose, and commitment, rather than a uniform pattern of ideological belief and social practice. Its *concern* is to embody and promote the reconciliation of humanity to God and each other that was exemplified in the ministry of Jesus. Its *purpose* and function are to infiltrate society with the Spirit of Jesus. Thus it is to function as a phalanx of what Clarence Jordan called the "God movement" ("the rule/kingdom of God"). It is to be a dynamic unit of the kingdom movement united by a common *commitment* and loyalty to Jesus Christ as Lord. Its goal is not uniformity but unity of purpose in a common cause. This, of course, raises the question of what Miraslov Volf calls "exclusion and embrace," but it sets quite different, non-sectarian lines of discrimination and demarcation.

It is perhaps understandable, then, that I find myself conflicted about the institutional developments in the Mennonite churches of North America during the recent decades. Not because I do not applaud broader fellowship and cooperation, but because I see so little authentic movement at the grassroots level to promote the personal-social goal of God's kingdom on earth. Instead of a *movement* connected by common spiritual and social concern based on the teaching and example of

Christ, Mennonites seem to be developing a *denominational institution* based on doctrinal uniformity and political accommodation. Yet at the same time I write this, I am fully aware that some organizational form of the religious group is necessary, and I applaud the efforts of colleagues to vitalize the institutional forms.

When my thoughts turn to God, I find that increasingly I am working with different metaphors than I did earlier. The metaphor of God as a transcendent king and controlling power of the universe, which so dominates our hymnody and popular thought, no longer seems satisfactory to me. As introduced in chapter 8, the technical term *panentheism*, which has become more widely used during the past half century, seems more adequate to image God's relation to the universe. It indicates that God's being and the universe are not conceived as absolutely disparate like they are in the Neo-platonic view of transcendence adapted by evangelical Christian theologians. On the one hand, panentheism affirms that there is a relatedness and interdependence, while at the same time it affirms that the universe accessible to empirical science is not all there is to God, as classic pantheism implies. God is not contained in or ultimately thwarted by the material universe. Christians know God as both the immanent person-creating dynamic and transcendent enlightening presence most clearly revealed in Jesus Christ.

The metaphor of parent—I still prefer "Father," which I have always limbically associated with my mother—still seems useful to me as a symbol of unindulgent guidance, approval, and comfort. But I find myself thinking more in the vocabulary of eternal Light and Life, the terms used in John 1:1-5. God is the indestructible Life and unquenchable Light of humankind. This unstoppable dynamic continues creating and enlightening personal spiritual life despite the darkness and violent opposition. And the great mystery is that this divine Energy operates nonviolently, not as a violent controlling Power. The God of Jesus Christ is the "God of Peace."

This brings me to peacemaking, where my journey has been from nonresistance to nonviolence, from sectarian nonconformity expressed in withdrawal from a violent world to an involved noncooperation and nonviolent action in and for that world. I take the truism that there is no real peace without justice much more seriously than earlier. I am convinced that Jesus meant for us to be *peacemakers* and not just *peaceable*. Salt, as someone has put it, is not intended to be stored in a saltshaker.

And this brings me to my changed understanding of Jesus and his relation to society, law, and the politics of forgiveness. I have for many years been impressed with the significance of the general concept of Jesus' humanity for a theological evaluation of his role as messiah, but I now begin to understand the significance of his Jewishness. He was a Jewish male fully involved in his society and culture, conditioned by its assumptions, wisdom teachings, and rabbinical traditions.

This, as I now understand it, has important hermeneutical ramifications for the interpretation of his message and example. The cross is not to be understood as an example of absolute nonresistance to systemic violence, thus requiring withdrawal from the world. Rather, working within the broad assumptions of the Jewish wisdom tradition, it models a strategy of non-retaliatory confrontation of social evil and violence. Obviously the politics of such a position will need to be developed in each local culture, but the basic gestalt remains unchanged.

All this brings me to a fundamentally different paradigm for understanding miracles. We are so dominated by empirical notions of reality that we forget that the definition of miracle is not necessarily limited to physical and material dimensions. Miracles, simply put, are acts of God that change the human situation for the better.

When I view Jesus within the strictures of his cultural conditioning, I begin to see that he himself is the embodiment or incarnation of miracle. Precisely his life, death, and resurrection are the miracle! Comprehending this through the inspiration of the Spirit, the writers of the Gospels represented his very entry into the world as a physical anomaly, which we in our empiricistic mindset have latched onto as the "miracle" of incarnation.

There are a number of miracles recounted in the birth narratives. One is the resignation of a frightened and uncomprehending Mary to God's plan when it meant her own social disgrace. Another is the willingness of Joseph to defy social tradition and stand by Mary in quiet confidence that God was at work creating a new thing! Still another and more profound miracle is that the boy Jesus should have survived in such a social situation to become the "Son of God"! Each story makes this same point—that this one born of Mary is indeed God's Messiah, as unlikely and impossible as it may seem! It is he who embodies the miracle of God's forgiveness; and through participation in his way of forgiveness, as St. Francis puts it, we are forgiven.

12

From Mennonite Fundamentalist to Critical Anabaptist: My Story

I was born in rural southeastern Virginia in a period of radical cultural change dubbed the "Roaring Twenties"—that post-World War I decade that preceded the stock market crash of 1929 and the Great Depression that followed. It was an era when men fell in love with their automobiles. When the cowboy rolling his own cigarette became an iconic figure. A period when women received the vote, cut their hair, took off their corsets,and scandalously shortened their skirts. But it was also the time when a strong conservative movement of fundamentalist and Pentecostal reaction to the new cultural climate was developing.

I was five when the stock market crashed. My earliest memories are of Depression times when my father, a plasterer, had a hard time finding work or collecting wages even when he did work. Then in 1932 Franklin Roosevelt was elected and introduced his new democratic socialism. I remember well when he was was elected and the fear that his NRA, CCC, and Social Security programs caused in conservative religious communities like the Mennonite colony in which I was born. We lived in a rural area where the paper was delivered by the mail carrier, and I brought in the mail the morning after the election. I remember Roosevelt's picture on the first page. It struck a note of fear in my own eight-year-old heart.

Our church leaders were much more comfortable with non-political Fundamentalism and anti-worldly Pentecostalism than with the politically liberal policies of the new administration. They feared that end-time prophesies of "anti-Christ" and the satanic number "666"—the "mark of the beast"—were beginning to be fulfilled. Many believed that these programs were the signs of "communist" influence. Conservative politicians were making lists of anti-Americans, and it was whispered that Mennonite leaders H. S. Bender and Orie O. Miller were on the list. I shall never forget the evening when Bishop George R. Brunk passed that information on to my parents and the other guests assembled while they were visiting in our living room at Eastwood.

I knew little of the new freedom that the cultural changes of the twenties introduced. As mentioned in the prior chapter, I was born into that tightly bounded religious community called "the Colony," settled by Pennsylvania Dutch Mennonites on a farmed-out plantation near Denbigh courthouse, located on the peninsula just twelve miles north of Newport News and Hampton. We were surrounded by a post-plantation, rural English society that had been jolted awake by the military development of the area during World War I and was just beginning to be important as an ongoing military center.

Although there were no physical fences or walls, as some Newport News citizens thought, the topographical boundaries as well as the moral and spiritual boundaries of the Colony were clear to me. I could have told you exactly which open fields and wooded areas belonged to it, where the Mennonite community ended and the "world" of non-Mennonite culture began, where I was comfortable and at home and where I was a "damned Mennonite." I grew up in two clearly delineated cultures, one represented by the public school and one by the religious community with its controlling center being the church.

It had not always been that way, but while I was growing up this church community was firmly controlled by the bishop, George R. Brunk, the first in a line of George R. Brunks, a towering, impressive figure determined to protect his flock from the onslaughts of the devil. As the occasion required, he confronted foes as different as Billy Sunday, the raucous revivalist preacher; the corrupt local sheriff's political machine; and the state of Virginia school board fighting for the rights of the Mennonite community.[1] And when the community telephone rang six shorts, the community emergency alert, we would sometimes hear his voice announcing, "Lock your screen doors. The Jehovah's Witnesses are in the area." In the community itself he dominated both the social and theological climate. So I cut my theological eyeteeth on a premillennial interpretation of the King James Version of the Bible as the infallible, literal word of God. The major problem with Fundamentalism, George R. used to say, was that it is not fundamental enough! We Mennonites kept the "all things" commanded by Jesus in the great commission (Matt. 28:19.)

From this restricted and sheltered beginning, my life has expanded and grown in the pattern of a chambered nautilus. I do not remember any major revolts, only in-process course corrections. It may be hard for those who have grown up in the Shenandoah Valley to believe, but my first major culture shock came when I entered Eastern Mennonite School as a high school junior in 1940 and had a roommate from Pennsylvania who wore a necktie. In all other respects, he was a quiet, conscientious Christian boy who would not even buy an ice cream cone on Sunday! I just could not put the two things together.

And my first theological divergence from Denbigh orthodoxy came when I returned to the college division of Eastern Mennonite School in 1943 to enter the Th.B. program. I began my course of study with New Testament Greek and Systematic Theology. Chester K. Lehman, who taught the latter, gave us a Mennonite adaptation of the "Old" Princeton theology, which embodied and defended Reformed orthodoxy. While he adopted a more Arminian version of that theology, which allowed for human free will, he did not modify its uncompromised nonmillennialism, which "spiritualizes" the 1000-year reign of Christ at the end of the age. That roiled premillennialists like Menno J. Brunk, who claimed it was a first step away from biblical literalism and opened the door to Liberalism. Brunk, who had been educated at the Dallas Theological Seminary, the center for premillennial dispensationalist theology, used to say, "If the literal meaning of the text makes sense, it is nonsense to make any other sense of it."

Instead of finishing my Th.B. degree at EMS as initially planned, I went to Goshen College for my last year and earned a B.A. in Bible, the difference being that a Goshen degree was an accredited liberal arts degree. Although I had to take mostly liberal arts courses to complete the requirements for a B.A. in one year, I became aware that Goshen was not the beehive of liberalism I had been led to believe. As would become much clearer in my experience later as a pastor, the differences between eastern and midwestern Mennonitism was far more related to their difference of origin in the Mennonite and Amish traditions, and in their acculturation patterns on the Eastern Seaboard and the Midwest frontier. This was a major step in expanding my view of the "world."

Going to Goshen in those days was tantamount to betraying the conservative cause, and to my great surprise I was asked to return to Eastern Mennonite School to take over Harry Brunk's high school history and government classes, since the college was expanding its liberal arts curriculum. Even though my degree was concentrated heavily in Bible, and I had not taken courses in history, government, or teacher education, I welcomed the unanticipated chance to become a teacher. Up to that time I had expected either to go into the ministry or to the foreign mission field, but a call to the ministry depended on being chosen by lot. That would have meant simply finding a job and waiting, and having broken ranks by going to Goshen College the wait could have been a long one!

I taught at Eastern Mennonite School from autumn 1946 to spring 1949, then I returned to Goshen to complete a seminary degree in Goshen Biblical Seminary. I fully intended to return to Virginia, but, as my mother-in-law used to say, "it was just not to be so." Sometime during spring 1949, Dean H. S. Bender stopped me on the sidewalk at the west end of the administration building and asked whether I would be willing to accept ordination in the Indiana-Michigan Mennonite Conference. I demurred that I had planned to return to Virginia, but he assured me that an ordination need not mean a permanent assignment in Indiana.

With that understanding I accepted ordination and an assignment at the Maple Grove Mennonite congregation, a small rural church in Topeka, eighteen miles east of Goshen. Little did I know that during that same time an investigation of the Eastern Mennonite School faculty was in progress that would have made my return there as a teacher quite impossible in any case. But that is a story for another time.

The year 1950 was a momentous one for my wife Ruth and me. We had been married spring 1945, while I was still in the Bible school program at Eastern Mennonite School, and had moved into a small second story apartment in Park View, just off the campus. We fully expected to finish the year at EMS, but an unplanned pregnancy prompted us to transfer to Goshen the next fall. Ruth was from Elida, Ohio, and had attended Goshen College, so moving in that direction for the birth of our first child felt comforting to her. Now in 1950 our third child was on the way, and I was finishing seminary with no prospects of a job that would support us. Churches were not yet supporting their ministers.

It was at this point that Dean Bender again approached me about the possibility of my teaching in the Bible Department at Goshen. Bender also inquired whether I would be interested in going on to graduate school, perhaps in Germany, a suggestion that greatly interested me.

After graduating from Goshen Biblical Seminary in spring 1951, I began teaching there that same fall. At that time the Bible department and the seminary were still integrated. Students in the seminary received a B.A. degree with a major in Bible after four years of study and a Th.B. the fifth. Since Bender was taking a sabbatical that year, he assigned me two of his Th.B. courses to teach—the Acts of the Apostles, Romans, and Corinthians, and, as was customary for new teachers, the Greek language courses. That year and the following one were especially stressful, since I was also pastoring at Topeka and often went out there two and three times a week. Given that pastoring was non-paying and the nine-month salaries at the college were low, I had to get a job over summer to keep a growing family alive.

In autumn 1953 I went to Princeton Theological Seminary on Dean Bender's recommendation. By then our twins had come along, so there was a family of seven to plan for. The two older girls, who were in elementary school, went to live with their grandmother Kraus in Denbigh (now Newport News), Virginia, and the rest of us moved into a newly refurbished seminary apartment at 21 Dickerson Street, Princeton, New Jersey. It was a fabulous and full year! Besides completing a masters program, including writing a thesis, I often preached in the Mennonite churches of Bucks County, Pennsylvania. Ruth got a part-time job, which she enjoyed, and with the apartment only a block from the library I studied at home as much as I could.

This was my first experience of genuine graduate work anticipating that I would be going to Europe to study church history if we could get the money together. But at Princeton I got a new vision for what I thought was needed at that juncture in the Mennonite church. For the first time I was introduced to the field of American church history and theology, and I came to realize that this was a missing piece in the academic curriculum in our college and seminary. We were concentrating on Bible and Anabaptist-Mennonite history but paying little attention to the religious culture we were living in. At that time, for example, the shelves of the Goshen College library did not contain books Bender and his colleagues considered "liberal," and theological analysis of American trends was virtually non-existent.

So I majored in American theological studies and did a thesis under Dr. Lefferts Loetscher, entitled *Dispensationalism in America: Its Rise and Development*, later published at his suggestion by John Knox Press. In the 1940s and 1950s prophetic interpretation was still a major issue in Mennonite theological circles. Bender, however, was uninterested and apparently unimpressed. To my knowledge he never included a review of my book in the *Mennonite Quarterly Review*. A few years later, when I returned from Duke University, I suggested to him that we ought to include a requirement in American church history in the budding seminary curriculum, but he remained quite unconvinced.

The Princeton faculty offered me a generous fellowship to stay and continue my study for a doctorate, but President Paul Mininger pressed me to return to Goshen. J. Lawrence Burkholder was finishing his degree at Princeton, and Goshen College was short on faculty. They would need to hire another teacher if I did not return, so they could not continue my study leave, which, of course meant they could not guarantee me a continuing job if I did not return. Since we were operating with virtually no cash reserves, and I was not yet on the tenure track, we had few alternatives.

The next three years were crowded with activity and tension. John W. Miller, who had been sent to study in Switzerland in preparation for teaching Old Testament at Goshen Biblical Seminary, returned that same year. His continuing connection with what had come to be called the Concern group (of which Irvin Horst, Paul Peachey, Calvin Redekop, David Shank, and John Howard Yoder were also members), and his undisguised espousal of the critical analysis of Scripture soon lost him the good graces of Dean Bender. I agreed with John's communal ecclesiology that identified the essence of church as "primary relationship," and together with him was involved in fostering the koinonia groups we considered the primary expression of the church. We sponsored visits by Bruederhof (English Hutterite) leaders to the campus and engaged in extended private discussions with them. We also organized a small communal group of faculty who practiced economic as well as spiritual responsibility to and for each other.

At the same time other theological and ethical issues were emerging. J. Lawrence Burkholder's thesis written at Princeton, which questioned the ethical relevance of the Hershberger-Bender position on absolute nonresistance, caused quiet but intense tension on campus. My own questioning of the doctrine of scriptural inerrancy, which to that time had not been openly challenged, caused uneasiness. Besides that, the popularity of the Billy Graham campaigns and the introduction of this emphasis into Mennonite circles by the George Brunk and later Myron Augsburger tent campaigns put great pressure on the seminary to be more evangelistic in its emphasis. We spent more than one seminary faculty meeting discussing the meaning and methods of evangelism, and Dean Bender sought rapprochement with George Brunk by helping to bring his tent meetings to a field just east of the college in 1952 and giving him a place on the college podium.

During these same three years the seminary faculty was debating the merits of discontinuing the Th.B. curriculum and developing an accredited graduate seminary program. Bender had decided that was the way to move, but not all of the professors fully agreed. Paul Mininger, who later became president of the college, was the most hesitant. He himself was a bishop in the church and very aware of the implications of such a step. With the use of the lot to choose ministers already in sharp decline—we were only beginning to use the word *pastor*—a three-year graduate seminary curriculum would be a big step in the direction of a professionalized and salaried ministry. At the college level, of course, it would require the re-organization of the Bible and religion curriculum as an integrated undergraduate program. I am convinced that the experience of these three years on the faculty was well worth the delay in my doctoral program.

In 1958, the year my book on Dispensationalism was published, I was given a major fellowship by Duke University to continue my graduate studies in American church history and theology, and this was followed the next two years by the newly established Rockefeller Theological Fellowship. I was particularly interested in going to Duke to study with H. Shelton Smith, who had recently published *The Changing Conception of Original Sin* (Scribners, 1955), a historical study on original sin in the American theological tradition. This was the period when the challenge to the old Liberalism by Karl Barth, Emil Brunner, and in America, Reinhold Niebuhr was at its height of influence. Along with my study of the American religious scene, I continued my interest in political theory and philosophy. These were the years of the opening civil rights movement, and I was caught up in the excitement of the local Durham developments.

The three years at Duke were a badly needed and much appreciated chance to escape my sectarian boundaries and the tensions that were developing at Goshen College in the last years of Bender's tenure. He was deeply involved in the formation of the new graduate seminary program growing out of the existing five-year Th.B. program, but he refused to relinquish chairmanship of the Bible Department. He apparently intended to have J. Lawrence Burkholder appointed as Bible Department chairman, but Lawrence left Goshen to teach at Harvard Divinity School. I was still at Duke University, and in any case, as Al Keim notes in his biography of Bender, he did not trust me to lead a college Bible Department independent from the seminary.[2]

My generation was caught in the middle of a major cultural and philosophical revolution that had impacted the Mennonite church already following World War I and continued unabated following World War II. Men like Bender and Orie O. Miller had brokered one stage of the transition and were loath to give up power. The power brokers in eastern conferences like Lancaster and Virginia managed to hold on for several more decades.

Those of us who chose not to be managed took our lumps, and the consequences were especially severe for those in the biblical and theological fields. But we realized that the generation of college students whom we were teaching faced a still more uncertain and unmanageable future than we had. For us at Goshen College, the crisis point in the changing cultural climate was 1967-68, the year of the Eugene McCarthy presidential campaign in the midst of the Vietnam War that drove Lyndon B. Johnson from office. From that point for the next few years students aggressively pushed for radical revisions in both the educational and moral disciplines on campus. The college was no longer to be accepted as in loco parentis!

In the early 1970s, we talked about the "generation gap" that had developed, which was likened to the gap between first-generation immigrants and their U.S.-born children. At Goshen College we were trying to introduce students to "Anabaptism" as a paradigmatic option to Mennonite fundamentalism when we were clobbered with the anti-Vietnam war protest and the "Woodstock" phenomenon. In this context our Anabaptist model of discipleship too often got interpreted as a variation on "Jesus Freaks," radical social protest, and communalism. Those students who rejected this interpretation tended to get lost in individualistic ventures or return to the denominational fold.

During those years student attendance at chapel and especially Sunday morning services dropped off precipitously. Some of us younger faculty, inclined toward more social activism and a less institutional view of the church as an organic body, tended to sympathize with them. Already in the 1950s we were forming koinonia groups we considered our primary church groups. We even held household communions, to the chagrin and anxiety of our elders. During the 1960s and 1970s, students also formed such koinonia groups and households, and (as recounted in a prior chapter), out of these independent but cooperative groups we formed a new congregation of small groups.[3] The congregation, known as the "Assembly," continues today as an authentic Anabaptist alternative to the traditional Goshen churches.

This represents what I might call the ecclesiastical concern that has dominated my life work. I was committed to a genuine ecumenical fellowship of believers, but it seemed to me that ecumenism needed to begin at the congregational level, not with institutional executives meeting in international conferences. It needed to begin with "the two or three together" with Jesus in their midst searching for existential answers to the personal and social questions of the day.

When I left the college in 1980 and went to Japan under the Mennonite Board of Missions, I still saw our basic task as attempting to form alternative Christian communities and not simply to convert individuals to Christ. For most Japanese people conforming to the Japanese culture, i.e., "being Japanese," provided their self-identity. Christianity was a "foreign religion" which might be added on to their unique Japanese identity, respected but not integrated into their sense of identity. My concern was how to help these people understand and experience the significance of Jesus for the formation of a new self-defining community—neither Jew nor Greek, Buddhist nor Christian, Catholic nor Protestant, Mennonite nor Lutheran; to experience what it meant to be "in Christ" as a new social reality.

During my nearly thirty years on the Goshen College faculty, I had taken a number of leaves of absence to take overseas assignments. Most of these had taken me to various countries in Asia. The family spent 1966-67 in India, where I taught at Serampore Theological College, the college founded by William Carey, Joshua Marshman, and William Ward about twenty miles up the Hooghly River from Calcutta. At that time Serampore was the hub of seminary education in India, since it held the independent legal charter which had been granted to Carey by the king of Denmark in 1826. When the British left India in 1948, Christian seminary education was organized under the legal umbrella of the Serampore charter. For me this was the beginning of cross-cultural experience that was to prove an irresistible pull in the years to come.

In the intervening years, I served on the Overseas Committee of the Mennonite Board of Missions and did a number of teaching and pastoral assignments under the auspices of MCC and various Mennonite mission boards in India, Taiwan, Vietnam, Philippines, South America, and East Africa—Ethiopia, Tanzania, and Kenya. Then in 1975, at the invitation of Takio Tanase, who had been a student of mine at Goshen College and was a leader in the Hokkaido Mennonite Church, we spent a full semester of my sabbatical in Japan on a teaching mission in the Mennonite churches. Besides the connection with Tanase, several of the Japan missionaries had been seminary colleagues and/or students of mine, so when we decided to resign from the college and pursue a cross-cultural teaching mission, Japan seemed a good location from which to operate.

I should pause to mention that this experience of teaching in many different cultures, often with an interpreter, had a major impact on my view of the Bible and how to communicate its message. Teaching the gospel of John in English from the Greek text to students from perhaps ten different language backgrounds, for which English was at best a second language but the only language they had in common, was a formidable challenge! And preaching to tribal pastors in the mountains of the Philippines through a chain of multiple translations by interpreters who knew only two of the three languages involved heightened one's appreciation for the priority and precedence of the Holy Spirit as both inspirer and interpreter of Scripture.

The Hokkaido mission was begun at a kairotic moment in the history of Mennonite missions. Although Japan was in an economic and cultural crisis as a result of the war, it was not an underdeveloped culture. The Christian message did not have the implicit motivation of economic advancement behind it to boost its acceptance. The Japanese people were well educated and relatively well acquainted with modern

Western culture. And under the virtually dictatorial direction of Douglas MacArthur, Japan was transitioning into democracy. Most of the original missionaries came from Goshen College inspired by the "Anabaptist vision" of Harold Bender, which fit this new democratic pattern very well. And with fifty years of Mennonite mission history in Asia behind them, they were determined to plant an indigenous Japanese church in the Anabaptist tradition.

My purpose for going to Japan was not to plant new churches, but to nurture churches that were just now coming of age. I was convinced that an "anabaptist" theology needed to be mission-oriented—what we are today calling "missional"—and speak existentially to the cultural situation. After some thirty years of studying and teaching historical theology, I now wanted to write such a theology—a theology aimed not so much at systematizing an orthodox theological thought pattern as at developing an authentic theological analysis and expression of the significance of Jesus for twentieth-century culture. Furthermore, I had become aware through my cross-cultural teaching that Western culture and its questions about Jesus and God by no means provide the only perspective from which to do God-talk. Indeed, the Western theological debate of the last two thousand years had almost become incestuous with inadequate formulations and answers giving birth to yet more controversial questions and answers.

What our Japanese churches needed, it seemed to me, was a critical analysis of Western theology based on an indigenous contextual interpretation of Scripture. After all, the scriptural narratives were not configured in the pattern of Greek dualistic categories. Indeed, there are aspects of Japanese tradition that are nearer to the ancient Hebrew culture than to modern Western culture. I felt that the Japanese should be free to understand Jesus as a full expression of the Divine reality without necessarily formulating it in the Platonic form of Trinity; and to explain the atonement in terms of their own shame culture, rather than the legal guilt culture of the West. They needed to understand and interpret God in the context of Shintoism's divine naturalism or Buddhism's mystical humanism rather than in terms of Greek dualism and transcendence. One church leader put it succinctly when he told me, "We know what the missionaries taught us, but to speak frankly it does not make good sense to us." And again he commented to me that for him with his Buddhist background "Jesus gets in the way of God." It was with this challenge ringing in my ears that I taught and wrote for seven years in Japan until summer 1987.

I still remember the customs officer who greeted us at San Francisco, or was it Seattle, on our return. He took a long look at my passport. As he handed it back said, "Welcome home." From our home base in Hokkaido we had traveled to many locations in Asia—the Philippines, Taiwan, Hong Kong, Thailand, India, and Australia—for extended teaching missions. We had come to dearly love our Japanese brothers and sisters and our mission colleagues in the work of the church, and Asabu Cho, Sapporo really had been home. Riding the train through the mountains between Sapporo and Obihiro, where I taught classes, was a genuine pleasure. The early morning train rides home where I would order a tube of potato crisps and a cup of very black coffee for breakfast were especially pleasant. But that "welcome home" in heartfelt American English warmed my heart! We were heading to Goshen to take up interim residence at 615 College Avenue until the house was sold and we moved on to Harrisonburg, Virginia, for our retirement.

We had come almost full circle. I completed that circle ten years later when my adult children and I buried Ruth's ashes in the cemetery of Warwick River Mennonite Church at Newport News, Virginia where I had grown up.

Notes

1. See David L. Zercher, "Between Two Kingdoms: Virginia Mennonites and the American Flag," *Mennonite Quarterly Review* 70 (April 1996): 165-190.

2. See my "The Professor and the Dean," *Mennonite Historical Bulletin* 62.1 (Jan. 2002): 6-8.

3. See the chapter in this volume, "The Beginning of the Assembly Conregation: A Theological Reflection."

The Index

The Author

C. Norman Kraus, Harrisonburg, Virginia, is a teacher-missionary-author, now retired, who taught for many years at Goshen (Ind.) College and Associated Mennonite Biblical Seminary (Elkhart, Indiana). He has served on administrative committees of the Mennonite Board of Missions (MMN) and the boards of Mennonite Central Committee, both International and U.S. In 1950 he was ordained to the ministry in the Indiana-Michigan Conference of the Mennonite Church and has served for a number of years as a pastor. A student of both Anabaptism and Evangelicalism and its origins, he is the author of *Dispensationalism in America* (1958), and editor of *Evangelicalism and Anabaptism* (1979) among other books.

He was born and raised in Denbigh (now Newport News), Virginia, and received his early education in the public schools, finishing college degrees at Eastern Mennonite College and Goshen College in 1946. He married Ruth Smith (now deceased) of Elida, Ohio, and together they raised a family of five children. During these years, he finished his seminary degree at Goshen Biblical Seminary (now AMBS), a Master of Theology degree at Princeton Seminary (1954) and a Doctor of Philosophy at Duke University (1961).

During his teaching years at Goshen College, Kraus accepted a number of overseas teaching and counseling assignments in Asia, Africa, and South America with various boards of the Mennonite Church. After thirty years on the faculty at Goshen College, he and his wife Ruth took an assignment with the MBM to serve the churches in Japan and East Asia and took up residence in Hokkaido, Japan. His Asian ministry was largely one of teaching and writing. He preached in churches, led seminars for pastors, participated in inter-faith dialogues and peace conferences, provided pastoral services for missionaries, and taught in a variety of seminaries and theological schools in India, Japan, and Australia.

Kraus' focus has not been simply on academic theology. While a teacher at Goshen College, he founded and directed the Center for Discipleship to encourage students and faculty to confront issues of social ethics and witness. He helped to begin a new type of congregation, called the Assembly, which emphasized life and witness together in "Koinonia" groups. From the early 1950s on, he was personally involved in the civil rights movement, and from the 1960s he played an active role in cross-cultural missions.

In addition to contributing chapters to scholarly symposia and many articles to both popular magazines and scholarly journals, Kraus is the author and/or editor of more than a dozen books. The latter include *The Community of the Spirit* (Eerdmans, 1974; Herald Press 1993, rev. and and enlarged), *The Authentic* Witness (Eerdmans, 1979), *Missions, Evangelism and Church Growth* (Herald Press, 1980), two volumes of theology entitled *Jesus Christ Our Lord*, and *God Our Savior* (Herald Press, 1987, 1991), *An Intrusive Gospel?* (Intervarsity Press, 1998) and *To Continue the Dialogue* (Pandora Press U.S., 2001).

Kraus and his wife Rhoda are at home in Harrisonburg, where they are active members of the Park View Mennonite Church.

Printed in the United States
50534LVS00005B/385-393